Always Freeing Beauty

Barbara Foster

Acknowledgments and Dedication

To my family: Thank you for loving me and supporting me, as I navigated through the world and made sense of myself. I'm grateful for you.

For my former college theatre professors: Thank you for being part of my experience, sharing unconditional love wherever you go, and for steadily sticking with me as I worked to grow into myself. You mean so much to me. I dedicate the stories "Unforgotten Gift," "Principia," and much of this book to you. John and Chrissy, thank you for being my friends.

Mostly, for my friends: This, my heart in words, is for you. I dedicate this book to you because you lift me up and you keep me going.

And for the artists that struggle with themselves, their work, and how it all fits in the world: This is for you, too.

TABLE OF CONTENTS

iii	Acknowledgments and Dedication
1	Letter to a Struggling Artist
3	Introduction

Family Foundations

12	My Pillars
15	In Memoriam

Incubator Life: On the Road to Freeing Beauty

20	Home
22	Wrestling with My Dark Heart
28	Crossing the Great Divide
36	Caged Animal
37	On the Battleground
40	Principia
43	L.A. Love Affair
45	Crawl
47	A New Chapter
50	The Incubator Time
52	Dancing to Forget
54	Renewing Colors
55	California Palms
58	Stuck in a Box
60	Becoming My Best Friend
61	Jungle Transformation
62	Releasing Fear
63	Florida
66	Mental Confessions

TABLE OF CONTENTS

69	For God
72	Reverse the Character
74	Rescue Me Not
76	Alignment Gives Us Wings
77	Letter from Heart and Soul
79	Negative and Positive Space
81	Self-Evaluation and a Call to Greater Action
83	My Oasis

Friendship and Connection

85	Connection of the Heart
87	Unforgotten Gift
90	Soul Connections
93	Hearts
95	Letter to My Best Friend
99	Mirror Friends

Creative Prose

107	The Bird in the Attic
110	Thrill of the Ride
112	Unleash Your Childlikeness
114	The Sun, the Moon, and the Stars
115	From Spinning to Walking
116	God's Masterpiece
117	Dare
118	Light Befriends the Darkness
120	Embrace the Dirt
121	I am Freeing Beauty

Letter to a Struggling Artist

October 2018

Dearest Reader:

Thank you for your letter. I see you. I know what you are going through. I understand it can be hard to produce the art you want. It can be a challenge to know if people are listening to you. I understand it can be so difficult to fight through feelings of self-doubt, self-loathing, judgment, inadequacy, and so on, but if you're an artist you <u>must</u> make art. You owe it to <u>yourself</u>.

If you have something to write, then write it. If you have a desire to spread color across a blank space, then by all means, paint with all the colors in your palette. Do it regardless of what the world seems to be saying. Do it regardless of how the world will look at it, read it, or perceive it. Just create! Do it because <u>you</u> love it wholeheartedly. Do it because it's what gives you the breath of life.

It doesn't matter if you put all your struggles into your creations and they come out sounding somber or looking dark. Sometimes that's needed. Sometimes that's where you are, and you know what, it's part of life. There would be no discovery or healing if there wasn't darkness before the light. There would be no way to amplify and celebrate the raw beauty of life, if there wasn't creation and art. So, it's okay to be and feel dark, but don't let that darkness become part of your identity.

I have had my fair share of dark moments, but I wouldn't want to trade them for anything because there was also so much growth during those moments. And my art, my ability to create, is what saved me through those dark times. Hold on to that, dear friend. You will be okay.

I encourage you to take a few moments to breathe. Get in touch with what is happening on the inside. What chatter is buzzing through your mind? What is your heart trying to say through all the noise? Are you allowing your impulses to be felt and seen, or are you suppressing every feeling that is calling for your attention? Listen. Observe and drink in all that is going on. Wrestle. Roll around in the dirt and the muck. Fight with your feelings, but don't let them define you. This is where your craft becomes your anchor.

When you step into the studio you should be ready to work. All creation that is done in the studio is for you alone. The world's problems will not be solved, but they can be voiced. They can be recognized, unveiled, and announced through the creation that you do. Creation is about storytelling and expressing. Creation is a raw and vulnerable thing. Creating art is how the truth of humanity is shown, and it is a tool that we use to understand how to be human. Do not berate yourself if the art you want to make is not flowing as easily as you wish. Being human is <u>not</u> an easy thing. Wrestling with your feelings, and essentially with yourself is not an easy thing. Therefore, creating a work of art should not be easy. Inspiration can spring up as sweetly as flowers in a field, but the work must be put in first.

Your art is needed. You have done nothing wrong by having dark feelings. I encourage you to use the wonder of creation to help soften the dark. Eventually, the light will come. It always does. Your art will be something that will not only be good for you, but will help others, as long as you create with commitment, love, passion, understanding, childlikeness, and above all, freedom. Tap into what makes you feel good. Dig into what allows the root of the dark to be better understood. Use <u>all</u> of it. Then share. Breathe and know that as long as you are making something that benefits you and the world, you are on a good path. Press on, my friend. I look forward to hearing from you sometime soon.

All the best,
Freeing Beauty

Introduction

Dear Reader:

Thank you for picking up this book! You are about to get to know me really well and learn about the family and friends that have impacted me. I also hope that you learn something about yourself, a friend, or gain a glimmer of inspiration through the stories I have shared.

The previous letter was written in October 2018. That was when I was a new college graduate, had moved from my childhood home to a totally different house in Florida, and was trying to figure out my purpose, all at the same time. This letter was created from a writing prompt. My mom had told me to write a letter to a struggling artist. It was originally signed "Apollo," the Greek god of music and poetry. It felt right to change the signature because when I wrote this it was a note to myself. I tapped into the deepest part of myself, my spiritual essence, which I call Freeing Beauty. "Letter to a Struggling Artist" has since been edited, but the message remains intact.

Over the course of the last four years, since college graduation in 2018, there has been no shortage of dark moments. Some moments I never thought I'd survive or get out of. There were many days that felt long, depressing, full of anxiety, and meaningless. As I started writing, and then writing more regularly, my days began to feel meaningful. I continuously worked to drop into the deepest part of myself. I worked to feel whole, and to find who I am as a complete being. Writing would free my soul and calm my restless heart. The above letter was the beginning of finding healing through my writing. I'm pleased to say, since writing this letter, that I've officially discovered the magic of creation. I've learned over the last several years that writing is truly my anchor. I sit down to write, either in my journal, or on my

INTRODUCTION

computer, and I feel anchored. It doesn't matter where I sit, as long as I've got something to write with. There's a profound grounding that happens. I wrestle with my demons, process the world, work to understand myself, and I heal.

I have often surprised myself during these serious writing sessions. When I write I find my talent, I fall in love with my heart all over again, and I understand my mind a little bit better than before. Also, when I write, the Divine and I immerse in deep conversations. This is when I get closer to Freeing Beauty. I'm grateful for this unique way that I can communicate with the Divine and feel connected to Freeing Beauty.

So, dear readers, since writing that letter in 2018 there has been a rich amount of searching, digging, and creating. I've been writing a lot. I created a blog so I could share my work more easily. As I did so my seriousness and passion for my craft grew. Inspiration began to flow even more. I created for myself first and then shared it with others. I'm grateful for all of this and I feel that Freeing Beauty and I are becoming one. Well, we already were a unit, but I had a lot of growing into myself to do.

I feel it is important to share the story of Freeing Beauty before any other stories are shared because this name launched my journey for deeper self-knowledge, better self-love, and overall creation, which is at the core of everything I write. This book is titled *Always Freeing Beauty* because that is what I've been striving for, particularly within the last several years. I work to always feel, see, express, and be Freeing Beauty.

The name Freeing Beauty is my spiritual name. It is a reminder of my spiritual essence. It is a tool to remember who I am, and who I become when I connect to the core of my spiritual essence. The name Freeing Beauty seemed to just appear out of thin air and landed in my lap when I was fifteen. I was taking a class that was about unlocking potential and grounding yourself in your purpose. There was more to it, but that's the gist of the class from my fifteen-year-old recollection. The instructor of the class, Sandy, was a man I had known my whole life. As I took this class I felt out of my element. It was painfully obvious that I was the youngest student in the class. I was among people that were perhaps thirty and older. So, it was comforting to have Sandy there because at least I knew someone.

I was mostly taking the class because my parents told me I should take it. They thought it would be helpful and good for me. I remember the class being interesting and sometimes fun, but as an extremely self-conscious fifteen-year-old I struggled to absorb a lot of the information. As I look back on the class today, remembering what it was about, I realize that perhaps I wasn't ready to ground myself in a sense of purpose, nor was I ready to unlock my potential. At the age of fifteen I wasn't even ready to wholeheartedly appreciate myself, so believing I had any kind of potential, or purpose, was not on my radar. That's perhaps why most of what we had done in class didn't really stick.

Getting a spiritual name would be one of the first profound tools that would allow me to get to know myself and discover who I've always wanted to be outside of my crippling self-consciousness. Each student got to have a one-on-one meeting with Sandy at some point during the week of the class. This is where questions could be asked, various aspects about the course could be discussed privately, and the student could work with the instructor to select a spiritual name, if they wanted.

My private meeting with Sandy was perhaps my favorite part of the class. I was sitting outside with him. We were sitting at a table, shaded by the patio umbrella. The pool reflected the light, and I enjoyed the moment. As I sat poolside with him, I enjoyed having this time to process the

INTRODUCTION

class.

Choosing a spiritual name was something that I felt I had to do. First because it was an option of the class, and I didn't want to miss out on something my parents were paying for. Second because as a fifteen-year-old I always enjoyed nicknames, things that allowed me to figure out my personality, or what others thought of me. Although I was aware that this spiritual name was not a nickname, I knew it went beyond that. I knew that it was not going to be like any quiz I might take on Facebook. Those quizzes never told me anything about myself, and they definitely didn't give me a clue of what others thought of me. I knew this spiritual name would be deeper than all of that. But mostly I felt I had to do this spiritual name thing because my parents did. Both of my parents had taken the class and had come back talking about spiritual names. I always wanted to be a faithful daughter and to please my parents. I knew they wouldn't be upset if I came back *without* a spiritual name but hearing how profound having a spiritual name had been for them, I felt that it was the right thing to do. I had no idea how profound this name would eventually become.

During this meeting we chatted about a few things and then Sandy opened it up to me. I was allowed to ask or say what I needed to. The spiritual name was the only thing on my mind. I felt I needed to at least begin to come up with one. Though I knew there wasn't any kind of pass/fail system, being the young school student that I was at the time, I felt that it was important for me to get a leg up on this spiritual name before I went home. I subconsciously thought that if I could start ruminating about a spiritual name and tell my parents when I got home then I would "pass" the class. Although I was also genuinely curious to explore this spiritual name idea for myself. So, when my instructor asked if there was anything I wanted to talk about, I remember saying something like, "I'm not sure about a spiritual name."

I felt strange asking for help with this and therefore didn't directly ask. Knowing Sandy, I trusted he understood what I was trying to say. However, I was nervous that he would say, "That's for you to figure out."

After I tentatively posed my question, Sandy asked me some questions to get an idea of what my spiritual name could be. Once I gave him a few quick answers he got very quiet. He definitely looked like he was pondering something. He looked away from me for a while. He was so deep in thought that I got worried that my mere presence was interrupting him. I didn't want to bother him, even though I knew he was thinking about my question. In an effort to tame my flight impulses, and not run away from this moment of silence, I looked down at my feet. I wasn't wearing shoes. The ground was warm under my feet, and I liked that. Then Sandy gracefully looked at me. He paused. I looked at him, feeling like looking away, but trying not to, and trying not to hold my breath.

After a pause, he said, "How about Freeing Beauty?"

The air seemed to become lighter, and warmer. I enjoyed the environment we were in, but I felt undeserving of something so beautiful. After all, this was the beginning of when I was desperately trying to understand myself and how I fit in the world. *Who was I to have something this beautiful and profound presented to me?* I thought to myself. *How could I take this suggestion without dropping it?* It felt too big for someone who constantly felt small.

Sandy was quiet and very patient.

Eventually I said, "Oh, I don't know. I like it, but I don't know. It's cool. I like the way it sounds, but I'm not sure."

Sandy gently smiled. He was calm and not looking for a right answer. He was in no hurry, and I was grateful for his steadfast presence. He said, "That's okay. Take some time to think about it. Sit with it for a while. Sleep on it." He reminded me that it was okay if later I wanted to change it. I was not bound to any name, or one that didn't feel right. This was helpful.

After that I thought about the name. I sat with it. I slept on it. I woke up with it and I wondered if it was really me. By the end of the class everyone wrote their spiritual name on their name tags. I revealed mine to everyone. Everyone's eyes seemed to sparkle upon reading my name. That kind of attention was a little overwhelming. I got butterflies in my stomach, and I felt like hiding under the table, but I stood my ground the best I could.

Once the class was over, I returned home to my family. I was now back at school and going about my usual activities. Some people at church who knew about Sandy's class asked me what my spiritual name was, and I told them. I told several people as time went on. I noticed that I would have to repeat myself and over-enunciate when I would share my spiritual name with people.

"I'm sorry. What is it?" people would say, leaning closer. Sometimes my mom would share it for me.

I'm sure it was my self-consciousness that made me struggle to speak up the first time and enunciate so that people could hear me, but it was awkward for me to share something like this with people. It was so new, deep, and different. I felt too young and too small. *I don't know myself,* I thought, *so how could I have a spiritual name that everyone needs to know? Why do they all light up so much when they hear it? Why can't I say it more confidently so that people can hear it the first time? What was that class even for if I feel even more out of place and nervous around people?* All of this weighed on my mind. I ruminated about this name, Freeing Beauty. It played over and over like a song that was stuck in my head. It eventually got very annoying. I wanted it to go away, but what's more I wanted to feel better about being myself. I wanted to feel good about being Barbara, but everywhere

I went I didn't like being Barbara. So, Freeing Beauty lingered in the back of my mind.

One day, a year or so after that summer, I went to my study skills classroom during lunch. There was no one there, except the teacher, who allowed her students to use the classroom as needed. I loved how empty and quiet that high school classroom was. I jumped on the computer and opened a Word document. I felt like writing. At the time I had no idea how profound writing was for me. I liked writing, but I didn't see it as a saving grace. It was just something I did sometimes. However, this name and the way others were perceiving it was really bothering me. I needed to shake these feelings. I needed to get to the bottom of all of this. In an effort to do so I started writing a poem called "I am Freeing Beauty." I really worked to try to relate the name to myself. I tried not to disregard it because I liked it. I wanted to hold onto the name, but I always felt like I could jump out of my skin, so perhaps I shouldn't try to hold onto the name. *Why have a spiritual name if I couldn't feel relaxed as myself?* I never felt confident enough in myself to not get anxious. I felt like Peter Pan desperately trying to stick his shadow on himself with soap. It was a real struggle for me to be a human being and one that was out in the world, fighting through all my feelings, and trying to keep myself from unraveling at the same time.

After I wrote this poem, I felt a little better. I felt better about this name. I was able to see how this name could work for me, but this lasted only a moment. As I fought with myself for the next several years, I fought with this name, too. *Who am I to be Freeing Beauty if I can't even be Barbara first? I'm not Freeing Beauty! I'm not pretty enough, or in all other ways good enough to be Freeing Beauty.*

And this is where, starting in my college years, writing, serious journaling, and crafting stepped in to help me work through all my emotions. Each time I wrote, talked to

INTRODUCTION

trusted friends, and wrote some more, Freeing Beauty would appear in my mind like a gentle, gorgeous butterfly and whisper to me, "Yes, you are. You see, you are!"

So, dear reader, the pages that follow this letter are more precious to me than anything on the planet, and I've compiled them into one book. These stories are not in order of how they were written, but in order of the trajectory of my journey. This is my journey home to Freeing Beauty. From each of these pieces I have written my way through depression, anxiety, heartache, longing, passion, joy, romance, and peace. I have written my way to a softer heart, one that is light and grateful. The pages that follow are my deep inner thoughts and feelings processed, explored, and realized. These pages are a personification and celebration of my craft. Thank you for reading.

All the best,
Barbara Foster

Family Foundations

My Pillars

My parents' careers always made me sound really good to my peers. Each year I would get excited whenever I was asked to introduce myself in the classroom. Each year I would delight in watching the eyes of my peers pop out of their head when I would say, "Well, my father is a Delta pilot, and my mother is an opera singer."

Cue cartoonish reaction. "WHOA! THAT'S SO COOL!!" every single person would say.

I'd smile slightly, enjoying their enthusiasm, and I was grateful that one of the several lines I had rehearsed came out well. If I had a dollar every time that I mentioned my parents' careers, I'd have a hefty sum of cash.

I always felt like my parents were celebrities whenever my peers would react the way they did. After sharing details about my parents' careers and anecdotes about my siblings, I didn't have anything else to talk about. My family was the most interesting thing to me. I was somebody when I talked about my family.

I could talk about my hobbies, or what I liked to do, but I was always afraid people would lose interest. *I'm not as exciting as a Delta pilot, or an opera singer,* I often thought to myself, *and I'm definitely not as exciting as a sibling that is always ready to make someone laugh with a crazy character.* Instead, I was the reporter, the storyteller, the observer of the family. That was the role I felt safe playing for a long time, but I would later discover there are many different roles a person plays in their life as they grow. I had a lot of growing to do, but my parents definitely helped to guide my growth.

Though my parents' careers were cool, there was more to them than what they did for a living. When I was at home, I saw them as my pillars. Mom and Dad, the greatest superheroes alive, ready to tackle the day with joy, love, and persistence. When I was a kid, even when I was reaching high school, my parents were like giants in my eyes. I admired them and adored everything they did to make my life feel like a charmed life. My parents, like pillars that stand tall at the front of an elegant building, supported the foundation they gave me that the Divine is my Ultimate Parent, and guide. That was what home was built around.

I saw clearly the love and friendship my parents had for each other. I was grateful that home, for the most part, was always a happy place. There was the occasional fight with a sibling. There was the common "he said"/"she said" bickering rally, but home was always my happy place, and it's because of my parents.

I owe a lot to the Delta pilot that worked tirelessly each week for thirty-one years, who was home on as many holidays as possible, took his kids out to dinner, watched countless romantic comedies with his daughters, kept up with after school activities, and attended as many concerts, birthday parties, and sporting events as he could.

I owe a lot to the singer who taught voice lessons from home, got kids to Little League practice, soccer games, choir concerts, playdates, school drop-off and pickup, cooked dinner every night, while helping kids with homework, piano practice, guitar practice, and got them ready for bed that allowed them to sleep at an hour that was as decent as humanly possible when you're a mother of four children.

A round of applause would not be a decent representation of my gratitude, love, and respect. A standing ovation wouldn't be enough either. If I did get a hefty sum of cash, I'd give that cash to my parents, plus any amount of money I had scraped together for myself. I'd give it all to them.

My world was always fast paced, but I'm grateful to have had a mother that kept the household spinning and a father that was ready to pick up whatever was dropped or forgotten. I hope one day to pay them back for everything they gave me.

As I grew up and as I look back now, a majority of the discord I felt at home was no one's fault. It was me. It was me trying to bend over backwards and contort myself to be what I thought everyone wanted me to be. This is not an uncommon feeling for people, but it's something that engulfed me for a long time. I thought that I had to change myself for my family, and for everyone else I knew. I eventually learned, and I'm still learning, that the one who really pushed me to be someone else was myself. I began to wake up from the overwhelming need to please others, and be someone else, when I saw my parents stripped of their superhero capes.

It might have made them feel weak, out of control, or something similar to that, when they showed vulnerability. However, as a kid it was such a relief to learn that Mom and Dad are human too. I will always be most grateful to have learned at a young age that parents, though they try to look put together, they are not always at the top of their game. You don't need to be ashamed or feel discouraged, dear parents, for you have given me a gift. I see your vulnerability as a gift.

So, this is retirement. You're not sailing around the world. You're not flying in an airplane or glider every day. So, you're not in a concert hall gracing the world with your voice or touring with an opera company that has sold out shows. Or performing in a Broadway production, or a local play, or any other adventurous thing you'd love to do right now. You're doing what's needed, and what's important. You're listening to the Divine that says, "Right now, you must be here. Right now, I ask that you take care of this."

Thank you for being responsible, principled people. We will continue to grow, as we navigate life. It might be frustrating, sad, and uncomfortable at times, but we will survive. As Helen Keller said, "Life is either a great adventure or nothing." My life has not been dull, or without adventure, and I owe that to you because you've allowed me to have experiences. For that, and much more, I'll always be grateful for you.

In Memoriam

I didn't want any more pets, especially a dog. When I was around four years old a Golden Retriever bit me and since that time I didn't want to go near another dog.

When my sisters would see a dog out for a walk, they would run up to it, and ask the owner, "Can we pet your dog?"

I would stand about a foot away from them. I would awkwardly smile and wave at the owner and wait for my sisters.

Whenever we would visit a friend who had a dog or take a walk around the park in our hometown of Westport, Connecticut, I would hear dog owners pitch their voices up to call their dogs. I would hear dog owners coo, and squeak, and contort their voices as they talked to their dogs. I told myself I would never sound like that. I would never speak like that to any child, and especially never speak like that with a dog. No way! Not me, ever! Well...there was some Higher Power that had a different idea.

When I was seventeen, having had a decent lull without any pets, my family decided to adopt a puppy. They did their research on what breed would be best for a large family. They prayed on how to go about the adoption process. Eventually they fell in love with a German Shepard puppy. He was a breeder surrender, who was in foster care through Good Dog Rescue.

I remember my mother sitting on the phone with the rescue place. After she hung up, she told everyone in the family that out of about thirty applications our family was selected to adopt Major, the German Shepard puppy.

While everyone in the family was excited, I was angry. I was annoyed, and a little scared. I didn't want a dog. *Dogs*, I thought, *that jump, bark, possibly bite, and make a mess. Another animal that will give us something more to fight about. No thank you!*

When the family had cats prior to this decision, my siblings and I would fight over who would clean out the litter box. I couldn't imagine the clean-up that would have to happen and the fighting that would ensue once we brought home a dog. However, I had no control over the situation. It was five thrilled family members against one cynical teenager.

On October 29th, 2011, the family piled into our big blue Suburban and drove about an hour or so to a random parking lot. After waiting around a while, a truck that seemed to be almost as big as an eighteen-wheeler pulled into the parking lot. In huge blue letters on the side of the trailer it read GOOD DOG RESCUE. The truck stopped in an open area. My family, including a crowd of other excited people, gathered around the truck.

Here we go, I thought to myself, *no turning back now. This is a big mistake, but nothing I can do about it. So, whatever...*

The truck trailer ramp came down. I could vaguely see among the crowd into the truck. Crates and cages piled on top of each other with different types of puppies in each of them. A man came out holding a puppy and a bright colored piece of paper. He yelled out a last name, and another, and many more. People were raising their hands and pushing through the crowd to claim their dogs. I felt like I was at a bizarre raffle. Then finally...

"FOSTER!" the man called, holding a very small, black puppy.

My siblings almost jumped out of their clothes they were so excited. My father pushed through the crowd. He took the puppy from the man. The little puppy had a bright red leash around his neck. My family went to an open area in the parking lot and took turns walking our new puppy. I hung back, watching everyone quickly fall in love, and gawking over this creature. They were already arguing and struggling to take turns with the puppy.

On our way home it started to snow, and by the time we got to our house the yard was lightly blanketed in white. Snow in October was just the perfect end to an already strange day. Once our puppy was home it was immediately quite an adventure.

He was taken to dog training classes, socialized at the dog park, and taken to swim classes. We learned various commands and the right voice tones to get him to understand what we needed. We gave him lots of treats and toys and outside time. He loved to play ball, particularly "keep away," but mostly he loved to be with his people.

Major grew on me slowly. My old heart softened as Major's heart remained open. As we learned to train him, I found myself pitching my voice up to call him. I would squeak, and coo, and contort my voice when I spoke to him. I felt foolish, and dumb. I felt as though I was playing some crazy-dog-mom kind of role.

One day, when Major was about eight months old, I had realized that not only had I grown to like Major, but I *loved* Major! To my surprise, eventually, the cooing didn't feel so dumb. It began to feel real. I realized it was authentic because it came from a place of pure love. I wasn't afraid to go to the dog park, or anywhere with Major. And what's more is that he loved more vulnerably and unconditionally than any creature I had ever met. That was inspiring to me! When I would get angry or sad about something, he would be a steadfast presence full of peace and love. That was a big deal. I learned the value of unconditional love and what it looked like. I learned so much from Major. He was a bright spot in my family's life, and a gentle giant with everyone he came in contact with. My heart is forever melted. So, here's to you, my dear Major Puppy.

When the world around you got angry, you didn't cower. You stayed with a presence that said, "I love you." When the world around you got sad and distant, you didn't argue with it. You stayed with a presence that said, "I love you. I'm here if you need me." When the world around you was full of energy, you didn't bark, bite, or jump. You were peaceful. You stood your ground with a presence that said, "I love you. Show up how you must."

From "Come!" to "Sit," and "Lie down," to "Good potty!" "Okay!", "Free dog!" and "Good boy!" you were a very good boy. It was a treat to share adventures with you. From Connecticut to Pennsylvania and back to Connecticut. From Connecticut to Florida, and on to Colorado. You had many long car rides, adventures in the snow, and lots of sunny days of fun.

Heart and soul, my dear friend. You impacted many with your bright heart, and tender soul. The natural way you expressed unconditional love towards me, dear friend, was healing for me. I would pet you and feel your heartbeat as you stood beside me panting after a good run around the yard. I would see you look around, then look at me with your auburn eyes full of light, and I felt so grateful to stand with a tender soul like you.

I love you forever. Thank you, dear friend, for being you. Thank you for being my brother. Your depth of character will always be remembered and cherished. You'll always be my Major Puppy! I'll miss you. Your Foster family will miss you. But onwards and upwards with lots of love. Free dog!

Incubator Life:
On the Road to Freeing Beauty

Home

Standing alone while the world speeds by. Standing alone while the world rushes past. The world races around, flits and floats. People, the world, drive and move. They trudge along and push through. They talk at fifty miles an hour and type even faster. They go, they move, and they don't stop moving. They know things, and see things, and say things. They go, and they go, and they go. I stand still.

I can't process my own thoughts. There's too much noise around me. I try to block out the noise with music that sounds pleasant in the moment, but the noise grows. Now there is noise outside, around me, and inside me.

I can't digest my feelings. There's too much feeling around me. I try to help someone else because it seems like that's all I can do. I'm worried that if I try to understand my feelings or let them out a little, then more chaos would be brought to the world. I don't want to be the cause of an eruption of chaos or discomfort. So, I get up and show someone I'm here. I grab as much self-esteem as I can carry and head out to the races of the world. Then it gets too hard. I listen to music to pacify my growing feelings and watch TV until my body shuts down for the night. Now there is feeling happening outside, around me, and inside me. I wake up and through the blur of social media I enter another day.

Standing...alone. Standing alone while the world seems to continue spinning. I am lost. I do not know the world, but I watch it flash by each day. I am lost. Disconnected from the world and out of touch with myself. I do not know what I mean when I say, "myself." Who am I? How can I be so out of touch? How can I feel so lost while still seeing the world around me? Why has this strange and uncomfortable feeling of being disconnected from everything become something that is so familiar to me? Frustration, disappointment, and outrageously annoying do not begin to describe how it feels to be disconnected.

Holidays come and go, but I still feel lost. The bright stories that play on the TV screen become temporary nourishment for my twisted stomach, my buzzing head, and my weary heart. I fit right into the world, the one that has no idea what the other feels, and I melt into the TV. While I watch the sparkling stories that someone else wrote I can forget about myself. I don't even have to know what "myself" means. I can just watch a made-up life on a screen, but when it's over I turn quickly to social media. Then it all comes back. The world that rushes by and moves too fast for me to process my own thoughts and digest my own feelings. The world that makes me feel so very lost.

Home. I want to go home. I want to feel at home. When? When will I be able to come home? When will I be able to really feel at home? When will thought become clear, and grounded? When will feeling become steady, and aligned with everything?

Though I stand alone among a world of chaos, I hope one day I won't feel alone because my head, heart, and body will come home. I will be home. But...I'm not home yet...

Wrestling with My Dark Heart

I have feelings about my feelings. I have feelings about a situation and how I feel about myself in the situation. I have feelings about a conversation, when I'm in a conversation, and how I feel I felt in the conversation. I have feelings about how I spoke in the conversation and what the other person may have thought of me. Though I may seem composed at times, and though I want to be composed all the time, I'm always boiling over with feelings.

Starting in middle school I not only boiled over with feelings, but they started to get hot. I would boil over with feelings and an intense heat would rise. This heat spread like a virus through my body. This heat that spread through my body would then pulse out into the world. These boiling over, hot feelings that were too hard to suppress would grow cold like ice as I realized that all my hard to suppress, boiling over feelings made people retreat, and step lightly around me. Because of this treatment the icy sadness would erupt back into a heat so outrageous that nothing felt good. Nothing made sense.

I would boil over about the boiling over feelings. I would boil over about the pulsing and about how that made others feel. I would boil over about how they'd react toward me. I'd boil over about the heat of it all and that I have boiling over feelings.

Is your head spinning? Do you feel uncomfortable as you read this? Yeah, me too. Somehow, I've survived through it. I've lived to tell the story. So, hang on while I share with you. Or don't. It's up to you.

Middle school to high school I fought with myself even further. It was already so intense, it couldn't possibly get worse, but it got kicked up about four notches as high school approached. Soon those high school days seemed to smack me in the face. Then for four years I became wildly self-deprecating as I pushed through high school. The boiling over, hot and cold feelings became harder to manage. There were no outlets that could help me channel everything sufficiently and quickly enough. Since there was no time for a decent outlet during the day I'd stay up until the early hours of the morning. I'd blow off as much steam as I could by listening to music, thinking about *everything*, and watching TV. I'd stay up until 2:00, 3:00, or 4:00 in the morning. Sometimes I'd stay up all night! I'd stay up until my body would turn off without my permission. From those early high school days, I completely abandoned myself. I surrendered to the intense thoughts and feelings. Sleep and downtime no longer existed.

  I thought that I'd get in trouble at the drop of a hat for just existing with a forever bursting heart. This would bring in a harsh winter. My heart a blazing wildfire and my face the picture of a dark winter. Tears would fall like icicles, as my heart and mind would burn together. As life and situations presented themselves so did the boiling feelings, and the boiling about the boiling over feelings. I would boil about everything.

  No wonder I struggled to breathe fully and with ease! I was suffocating myself with all this emotion. I was strangled by the boiling over feelings about the world, and about people. I was sinking under the weight of everything. It never seemed to end.

  Since the beginning of my primary school days, I wrestled with myself. I've fought with God. I grappled with the greater good, love, joy, and with life. With every passing year I would scare more people and friends, and love seemed harder to hold onto. Eventually, death seemed to tempt me. I thought about and played with the idea of what that would do for me. These ideas of death turned quickly into suicidal feelings. Then my ice cold, fiery heart got dragged to college.

Simultaneously things got harder and so much better. Although at the time it felt like things just got worse. Love felt more distant, God made less sense, and the boiling feelings burned me alive. I would often wish I could be a robot so I wouldn't have to feel anything. Then I would be able to fit into the tame world, but by college that seemed impossible. Death became harder to escape from.

While I fought with this, I slowly found things that kept me afloat, things that taught me how to breathe, things that taught me how to love, and things that saved my life. One thing that did this for me was theatre. My professors, although they are not superhuman, or superheroes, they were my heroes. They showed me all the avenues and possibilities of theatre. They met me where I was in the dark, and said, "Hey, kiddo. You're alright. Take a breath. There's more to you than the dark." They taught me how to open up to love, how to love others, and myself. They talked me through why I needed to be kinder to myself and love myself as it related to my schoolwork. They listened to me, and I felt heard on a deep level, a level I only thought existed in my dreams. And they saved me by expressing inexhaustible, unconditional love, but most of all they showed me how I can save myself.

I soon made new friends who were just as wonderful. There were many people that took me under their wing and who guided me to joy and a better version of myself. I wanted to marinate in all of it, but I couldn't. The kindness felt like a hoax. I was hyper-aware of how some were uncomfortable by how I showed up and all I was wrestling with. It was confusing to my ego why these lovely people were standing by me. I would remember past looks from people, some that may have lasted for only a moment. I remembered things some would say in their discomfort, some things only said once. These voices and glances played in my head. They became weapons. I would bring the past into the present and the future. I relived it and it would distort the kindness that these new people were expressing.

I would get confused. I would get more depressed. I would boil over about all the heavy feelings I experienced and the kindness I saw others expressing towards me. *I do not deserve this,* I thought to myself. *Why couldn't they see that I'm a menace to society? What made them want to stand by me?* I wondered to myself.

I would often ask others what they thought. Some didn't understand why I needed to ask and in my continuous asking they would soon leave. I would understand that. Others wouldn't understand why I needed to ask and in my continuous asking they would stay, and perhaps they'd get closer. This I did not understand. This made love even more confusing, and I wrestled with love even more.

My mind exploded with questions. *Why do they love me? Seriously, why? Why do they stay? Why are they sometimes uncomfortable by my actions, but they stay? Would it really be heartbreaking if I gave into the temptation of an early death?*

I wrestled with the very young child my parents would tell me I used to be. The little girl that would sit on the bow of Daddy's boat and laugh as the waves would splash the side of the hull. The little girl that would run on the beach, fall into the sand and without brushing it off would keep running. I didn't know that child. I couldn't believe that I had once expressed such joy and freedom. I fought with that younger version of myself and the menace I felt I had become. It didn't make sense. But mostly it didn't feel good.

I tried to control all the feelings. It hurt and ate away at my energy. Somehow, though, I made it work. In public places, like the classroom, the bathroom became my safe zone. When the thoughts were exploding inside my head like fireworks, the emotions rising like lava, my efforts to suppress it all would begin to burst at the seams. When the firework thoughts would get louder, and the icicle tears would begin to sting, I would calmly ask to go to the bathroom.

It was always a relief when I had the place to myself. Since there was so much ice and fire inside me, and I felt pressure to get back to where I was expected to be in a timely manner, I could never release all the feelings completely. But after letting some of it out I was able to be a semi-functioning human for the duration of where I needed to be. Though my mind still filled with questions and ached for answers, the boiling was capped. I tried to seal it for as long as I could, until I was able to be alone again.

Teachers and other adults might think I was sweet, shy, and quiet. I'd lose my voice when I would speak to them, or even just standing in front of them I would quake in my shoes. Always afraid that I'd get in trouble for being me, and for having big emotions. I did not understand how these people thought I was quiet, or shy, or sweet? Seriously? Everything inside me felt so very loud. Why couldn't they see that? How was I not able to show that? For a long time, I used to berate my acting and performing abilities, but as I write this now, I guess I've been a great performer all my life.

I felt that some friends and family were uneasy around me because of my intense feelings. As I would gauge their feelings and how my feelings made them react, I would get lost in the frustration of how I felt like I was too much. I would gauge every look and hang on every word. I would compare and measure myself against friends, peers, family, and their body language. I was in the fight of my life.

I can tell you that the person I'm writing about is not the same person who is writing this. I have come a long way. Though I may feel these experiences as I write them, I can no longer go back. The past no longer thrills me.

During my college years there was something else that started to really save my life: writing, journaling, and the brave souls who were willing to be with me while I scribbled in my journals. They did not try to fix me. They saw my wrestling and raised me a healthy debate. Their body language, smiles, and steadfastness said, "No matter how hard you push, or fight with yourself, I will be here. You can never scare me or push me away. I have signed up to be your friend. Deal with it. Accept it. You can't make me go anywhere."

As the temptation of surrendering my life to death grew, and I asked questions about it, those same brave friends answered with steadfastness once again. And so did my professors. They constantly reminded me, and encouraged me, "We see the life inside you. We want to see more. We cannot save you, but don't break our hearts. Please. Do not give up your life. Our lives have been made richer because you exist as you are. We want you to do well and to live a life that's full. Please don't end it. You will get through this, and we are here for the long haul."

I hated taking baby steps in my life because it made me feel twice as weak. I wanted to make an immense amount of progress immediately, and passionately hated that I couldn't. Though I felt this, I knew that the little things were not nothing. Here's how I figured that out.

The little moments of encouragement from friends and professors meant everything to me! While I was working to convince everyone that I wasn't worth being seen because I felt like I was too much, too emotional, and too dark, my friends and professors ever so gently tapped at my light. They got to know what I liked, what made me tick, and how to pull me back to Earth when I would get boiled in my own feelings. They saw me drift in thought and brought me back to reality, and to the good. They requested I keep things simple, and not be so hard on myself, but they didn't treat me simply. I saw the love they had for me reflected in their eyes, and I saw their hope for me too. I never felt like a frail child when I was around them, and eventually I began to believe it for myself.

I was very unhappy about graduating from college

because I wanted to be a totally different person, and I wasn't. Once I got used to being in college, with all the care I received, it was painful to leave. It was painful to have to brave the world, as myself, on my own, but I've written, processed, and written some more over the course of four years. These last four years I've processed not only five years of college, but who I've been, how I've behaved, and how others have felt about me and my feelings, over the course of about eighteen years. Due to the intensity of all my experiences, how much has happened over the years, and how quickly life has moved, processing it all has been slow.

As I've worked through all of this, I have grown into a more mature version of my lively childhood self. I'm starting to come back to joy, to freedom, and to harmony. I'm embracing love and life. I'm starting to enter the land of the living, and above all I'm starting to find peace. I will never stop delighting in this newfound peace, and I will forever express my profound gratitude for the professors, the friends both new and old, and the family members that never judged the dark for a moment. Instead, they stood with me in the dark. By digging for the light in me they allowed me to be my own savior.

Now that I'm coming home, I want my friends to know that I'm here for them. I see their light and good nature. I see their beauty and profound ability to love. I love them for everything they are and everything they will become. Though I will always be working through my boiling feelings they will not deter me from being grounded. I am grounded for myself and for my friends, always. So, give me what you've got that's messing with your mind. Give me what you've got that's overthrowing your heart. You can't scare me. I'm here for the long haul.

Crossing the Great Divide

There has been a bridge intersecting childhood and womanhood. For a while my body has been sitting on the womanhood side of the bridge. It has taken my mind and heart a little while longer to cross the bridge. Body has been sitting on the other side waiting and waiting...and patiently waiting. Mind and Heart stood on the opposite side. Heart clung to the railing of childhood. Mind stood behind her.

"I can't do this!" Heart called to Body.

"Please just come!" Body yelled back. "I promise you'll be okay."

"It's not safe," Mind insisted.

"Yes, it is safe!" Body said. "I've been safely waiting over here for forever. Womanhood will not kill you. So, get a grip!"

"I do have a grip!" Heart shouted.

"On the childhood side of the bridge," Body scoffed.

"Yes! Of course. The best side of the bridge." Heart chuckled nervously, on the verge of tears.

"Uhh...we can't do this!" Mind hollered.

"Yes, you can!" Body yelled. "You just cross the bridge. Childhood and adolescence will be in your memory, but you cannot stay in the past. So please take a step forward! I need you!"

"You need me?" Mind inquired.

"Yeah! I need you to make wise choices for me and for us," Body said, "choices about what we eat, when we sleep and the person we want to become. We are a complete being, but we cannot function if we don't act like a unit."

"Do you need *me*?" Heart asked angrily, feeling jealous.

"Yes. Of course!" Body said. "You keep things going with your big dreams and creativity. You pump life into the system. You are a big part of the unit, but you must cross the bridge into womanhood."

Heart clung tightly to the railing of childhood, "Okay, but I don't feel like a woman. Can I cross the bridge and still be a girl?"

"You could," Body said, "that's fine if you think of yourself that way. Technically, though, you already are a woman. For several years you've been a woman whether you feel like it or not. However, I need you, and you too, Mind, to cross the bridge. I can't live life without you."

"No, no, no, no!" Heart slammed on the railing. "I need to stay here!"

"Why?" Body insisted.

"Uh, it's not safe!" Mind repeated. "You see, the bridge is made of wood and if the wood breaks, then we could fall through. Then we'd have to run and try to jump off the cliff to cross to the other side. That's even more unsafe. So, we'll just stay here. Sorry!"

Body tensed. "Oh my gosh! If you cross the bridge then you won't have to jump across the cliff. So just cross the fucking bridge! The world is moving along. Life is moving along, and I can't wait for you losers anymore!"

"NO!" Heart screamed.

"WHY!?" Body screamed back.

"Because!" Heart yelled.

"Because why?" Body hollered. "Why? Why can't you just cross the fucking bridge and help me out?"

"Because I'm not good enough! Okay? I'm not good enough to be a woman. I can't do it! There's too much expectation. There's too much responsibility, pain, heartache, and irrational hope. I'm just never pretty enough, hardworking enough, and in all other ways good enough to be a woman. So, no!" Heart faltered, tears streaming down. "I won't cross the bridge. I can't cross the bridge."

The breeze swept up the leaves and woke up the trees. Heart still held the railing, but she couldn't stand anymore.

Body took a breath for Heart and herself. Now she understood. She took another breath and said gently, "It's okay, Heart. You can be scared. I'm scared too. It's scary being on this side without you, but I had no choice. Growing up was just something I had to do, but I'm deeply malnourished, tired, and bored. I need your love, Heart! I've missed you so much. Mind, I miss you, too. Please cross over."

"Uh...I don't know." Mind hesitated. "I can't leave Heart alone right now. I miss you too. It would be nice to be a unit, but I'm not unit material. I mean...I mean I could be, but I just can't. I mean... I feel similar to Heart. I'm not smart enough to be a woman, confident enough, or fast enough. I'm just not cut out for it. I'm not fully equipped. I need to know so much, preferably everything, before I can think like a real woman. One who's mature, who can make wise choices, one who doesn't get flustered easily, or who cowers at love, and life. I'm sorry. I'm afraid I'll never be able to live up to the standards of womanhood. Very sorry."

Body sat motionless, staring blankly across the bridge. The water below sparkled and reflected pockets of light. The clouds rolled over the blue sky like a cartoon and the breeze continued to play with the trees.

Heart and Mind commiserated on the childhood side for a while. They had outgrown this side of the bridge long ago, but they could not bear to cross the divide. They wrestled with themselves and each other for years, every once in a while, calling across the bridge to Body to apologize.

"We're sorry!" they said.

Exasperated, Body yelled back, "Yeah! I bet you are!"

"We are!" Heart said.

"Umm...we just need more time!" Mind added.

"You said that four years ago!" Body clenched her fists. "You say that every damn year!"

"More time...please!" Heart said helplessly.

"One day I will be dead," Body said, "and in fact I

could drop dead anytime now. So, by all means, just stay stuck on the other side. I don't need you. It's fine!"

At some point each year Mind would force Heart into a serious conversation. They'd look at Body on the other side, lying flat on her back, looking up at the sky, motionless. This year the conversation was harder to ignore.

"Heart," Mind began, "each year Body's condition gets more serious. Her need for attention — wise, mature, balanced, loving attention — becomes more evident. Life *is* moving along. It has been for a long time. Do we really want to keep coasting through the world like this?"

"No, we don't," Heart said reluctantly, "but..."

"But what?" Mind wondered.

"But it's just..."

"Just what?" Mind urged.

"It's too hard and scary and hard, and I just don't want to do the work."

"But you do want to do the work," Mind said. "I know you want to. You've wanted to for a while."

Heart heaved a sigh. "I want to appear less childish and more grown up to others. I want to feel and be authentic without feeling like it's dumb, or that I'm small or that the space I take up in the world isn't a waste. I want that so badly, but being a woman just feels wrong. It feels too big for me. It feels far-fetched. The word itself just doesn't sound right or feel right coming out of our mouth."

"I get that," Mind said. "I can't even think the word without cringing, but womanhood is here. According to our birth certificate we are well into...you know, womanhood."

"Ugh...I know! I know. I know, but also no!" Heart exclaimed. "It's too much. It's all too big. I know we've neglected Body for...years. I feel really badly about that but crossing the great divide could be a disaster. No, actually it *will* be a disaster!"

"Heart," Mind said, sitting close, "it's already been

pretty close to disastrous. I mean look at Body. She's not doing so well. Feel Body. Get quiet for a second. How does Body feel?"

After a moment Heart jumped up and started pacing. "She's really hungry, unsatisfied and barely hanging on, but you know, somehow she seems to be kind of fine, so let's just go."

"Go? What?" Mind said anxiously, grabbing Heart. "Kind of fine? Is that what you just said? That's not okay, Heart. She is not fine, alright? She's not even kind of fine. And you know what, I'm not kind of fine either. I can't even think straight I'm so tired. And *you* are definitely not fine. You've been all over the place for years. You know, now that I think about it, I have no idea how we have survived this long! Some friends have said we're strong, but I don't know anymore. How did this happen? How did we get here? Where are we exactly? Nothing makes any sense anymore!" Mind began to cry.

"Whoa," Heart said, "wow. You are tired. Why don't you just sit down and watch this movie, and I will be right back."

"Wait! Where are you going?" Mind said in distress. "Don't leave me here alone!"

"I won't. I mean, I'm not! I'll be right back. You watch that movie, and I'll be back before it's over." Heart walked to the bridge.

She looked at the sparkling water, the sky, the clouds, the light that danced down below, and Body looking haggard on the other side of the bridge. Heart sat down. She sat quietly for a while. She felt the weight of her emotions, of Mind's many thoughts, and of Body's exhaustion.

"I'm really sorry," she whispered. "I don't know why I can't get it together. I know lots of hearts that have managed to beat from childhood to adulthood with no problem. They may still get scared, but they seem to be able to do things without getting sucked into the dark. And if they do get sucked into the dark, they are really good at not looking defeated."

Rolling over to face Heart, Body said, "How do you know that?"

Heart looked up and stared straight at Body from her side of the bridge. She replied, "It just feels that way. Everyone knows when I'm scared, or distressed, or uncomfortable. I make it so painfully obvious, and I hate it. Other people seem to just mask how they feel. They paint a big smile on their face and tell me to be happy too. So, I don't want to cross the bridge if I have to fake it until I make it, or practice inauthenticity."

"So don't," Body said, sitting up. "I like the way you beat. There's nothing wrong with the way you are."

"Thanks," Heart said shyly. "But I don't know...there's still so much more...that holds me back. I wonder if I'll be strong enough to last through a full-time job for more than a few months, or take care of a future house, or even an apartment, and the bills, and make sure to get enough food, but not too much that it spoils. I wonder how to do all that and maintain relationships in life, especially when they are so far away. I wonder how every woman on screen, or actress on stage, or women in business find the strength to get up each day and go to work. How do they do it?"

"I don't know," Body said. "I guess they just really want it, or really need it, so they just do it. Sometimes you just have to do it. Like eating, for example: sometimes you just have to put some kind of meal together and eat it. Sometimes you just have to get in bed, close your eyes, and sleep. You just do it."

"Okay, okay, geez!" Heart snarled. "I get it. I'm really sorry I abandoned you for so long, but facing you, Body, meant having to cross the bridge. I just couldn't do it. Sometimes I can't even handle being a girl!"

"Would you rather be a boy?" Body asked timidly, "I mean, I guess...well, it feels a little late for me, but I could get surgery if you wanted?"

"Oh, no! No. Whoa, no!" Heart exclaimed. "Please don't do that. That's not necessary! Like at all! I like being a girl. You don't have to change, Body. I mean, sometimes I wish you had slightly bigger breasts and that you weren't so tall."

"What's the matter with small breasts and being tall?" Body observed herself uncomfortably.

"I just don't like it."

"Heart!" Body exclaimed.

"And sometimes," Heart said, gently, "I wish you didn't have to go through a reproductive cycle."

"Oh. Yeah. I wish that too," Body said.

Heart said, "But mostly I wish I wasn't so embarrassed about it."

"You're embarrassed about it?" Body asked.

"Yeah. I am. I'm embarrassed about how I've shown up so far and many other things. I wish I wasn't, and I wish I hadn't been so childish, slow, and all over the place." Heart sighed. "But I was, and I can't take any of it back. That sucks. It really sucks!"

"It does suck, but what are you going to do? What else can you do? You can't go backwards."

"I know!" Heart said impatiently.

Body didn't take offense. She shrugged it off. "And you can't stay where you are much longer. So, where does that lead you?"

"Ff...forward," Heart said, cringing.

"Yeah," Body said, "just one step. One step forward. That's all it takes."

Caged Animal

Oh, to wrestle with yourself until you feel like a caged animal in your own skin. Oh, to wrestle with yourself so intensely that you become the cage and the animal all at once.

If only it were appropriate for humans to act like animals when strong emotions enter in. Some do. Some throw fits in public, but most try to tame their animal-like emotions behind closed doors.

Does it help? Are the emotions sufficiently tamed? Or does the cage start to feel tighter? Does the animal inside you grow? Does it want to growl and roar at the top of its lungs? Does it want to bare its teeth and shoot looks like daggers? Does that make you feel better about yourself? How does the world feel about it?

Is there a key to the cage? Is there a friend to come along and bend the bars, to rip apart the cage and bail you out? Or do you have to be your own friend? What if you never become your own friend?

Oh, to wrestle with yourself until you feel like a caged animal in your own skin. Oh, to wrestle so intensely that you become the cage and the animal all at once.

Oh, to not know where the key went. Oh, to not know how long it will take to find the key. Or to accept the painful fact that it's right in front of you. And so...the caged animal roars on.

On the Battleground

It started with the breath. Every emotion and thought that buzzed around like atoms would cut the breath off. As the breath became shallow, tension grew. Emotional tension, intense thinking, but most of all Body became very tense.

Raised shoulders, clenching in the stomach, slouching that hurt, a tightly clenched jaw, and Body fought for breath.

Then the emotions ran wild and took off in every direction. They were untamable. They were untrainable and they walked all over me. While Body tightened further, and Heart ran wild, Mind was riding its own roller coaster.

"Where do I belong in all of this?" Mind would ask. "Who really wants to connect with me? Is there such thing as deep connection or will it always be surface level?" Mind never stopped asking questions and trying to put everything together into one neat and complete puzzle. Mind was always disappointed at how quickly the uncompleted puzzle would collapse.

"Everyone looks like they know what they are doing in life, and if they don't know what they are doing then they are doing a really good job at hiding it," Mind would say. "Everyone seems to know how I should live my life. They never really know how I feel, but clearly it doesn't matter because it's not about how I feel. It's about doing work. So FINE, I'll do work! I wish I wasn't such a mess. I want to feel connected. Why can't I fit in? Mom says that Grandpa said, 'Don't force parts.' I think that's cool, but I don't know how else to make it work the way I want it to unless I force it. This puzzle needs to come together or I'm going to break. I *need* to fit! If I don't fit in, then I'm nothing. If I'm not a stellar academic, then I should not be in school because I'm too stupid to be in school. Creative expression only seems to be one small part of my overall report card, and the report card seems to be how I'm defined by everyone. If I don't get excellent grades adding up to a high-grade point average, then it appears I will *not* be who I'm expected to be. I'll amount to nothing. I *need* to be somebody."

Mind, Body, and Heart tried to make everything work as individuals. Soon an intense and internal war broke out. Small remarks from siblings, critiques from teachers, and every stranger's glance became weapons in my arsenal. I'd pull one out, and another, and a few more. Each weapon would point out, "See, this is why you suck! This is why you will never be enough. This is why you can't...you won't...you aren't. This is why you shouldn't even try. Don't try! Just give up!"

Finally, Mind would cry in anxiety, "I wish I was a different person." This was its deepest plea.

Tears would run like waterfalls. Rage would fill the whole room like a volcano and cause things to get thrown, and possibly to break.

The breath fought for its life and Body lost its appetite.

The battleground was now completely torn apart and scorched. Mind, Heart, and Body sit in their respective corners looking at each other, feeling battered, exhausted, and at a loss for what they need to do to work together without fear.

"Now what?" Mind questions. "I dedicated myself to trying to fit in. Now that it's over I don't know what to do with the rest of my life."

Heart croaks, "I don't know...but whatever we do... please don't make me cry anymore. I'm SO TIRED! I can't hate anymore. I don't want to be self-destructive anymore. Nothing feels good. I want to feel good! Fitting in, sure, but is that as important as feeling good? I forgot what joy feels like. I don't remember going through life without some kind of weapon in my hand. I feel as though I have died and come back to Earth multiple times, and each time I get weaker. Self-destruction, heartache, and loathing weaken me. I need someone else to take the reins. Revive us, please?"

"Glad to have your input," Body says. "All I've ever tried to do is survive. Mind, Heart, you guys have made it so hard to just survive. I've been wondering when you both were going to shut up and listen to me for just a moment. There is nothing wrong with me, nor has there ever been anything wrong with me and that's a freaking FACT! All I need is for everyone to put down their weapons. I need water, and food, and a shower. Then, Heart, you can be as free as you are beautiful. Do your creative work and express yourself! Nothing is stopping you. Mind, if you let us do that you will see we're okay. You're not stupid. You function just fine. You've been overworking yourself. There's no need for that. We can work together if I get food, water, and sleep. There's really no room for fear in any of that. In fact, if I get what I need, then Heart can get what she needs, and you, Mind, can get a break. Breathe. Mind, take a breath. Heart, take a breath. It's time to practice surviving and once we do that, *as a team*, then we can thrive together!"

It's quiet for a moment. For the first time in years Heart discovers her breath. Mind tries to breathe and relax. Body starts to let go of bottled tension with every deep breath.

"Go together," the Universe whispers. "Go gently together. Stand up together. Take one step together. Breathe. Breathe. Breathe. Love yourself, love each other, love Me... and thank you in advance. Once again, take it easy. Go gently together."

Principia

I like to say that college is where I grew up. It's where I went from being a teenager to a young adult. It's where I learned the fundamentals of theatre performance, the fundamentals of writing, of friendship, of what it means to be a student, how to take care of oneself, and the basics of being present with the Divine.

Each day for five years I was put to the test. I was very fortunate to have professors, friends, and loved ones that were not afraid to walk into the darkest of places with me. I would spit out every dark thought I could until daytime turned into the blackest of nights, but there was always someone there to catch me, to take my hand and show me how beautiful the light is. And that it will always be brighter than the dark.

College is the place where I learned the power of making my own choices. I learned that making my own choices is a privilege, and an act of self-care. I learned that making choices is not only the adult thing to do but the caring thing to do, and with care comes love.

I learned I could choose to starve myself or make myself a meal. I learned that at the hours most go to sleep I could allow myself to rest, too, or stay up until the sun came up. I learned that while the sunrise is beautiful, it is easier to enjoy it when the body has had proper rest and homework has been completed. I learned the value of time management, responsibility, taking ownership of oneself, being present, and the amazing healing power of theatre. I'm forever grateful for the brave and beautiful theatre professors that allowed me to be myself and that stood beside me as I wrestled with my ego. I learned how to shoot my ego in the foot, so it won't get up and start another raid on my soul.

As I fought through everything I'm not, I simultaneously began to embrace the tools I was given. These tools slowly filled in the negative space, the darkness, and I soon began to feel like positive space, beautiful light. I learned the power of gratitude, even if it was something I could only feel, rather than articulate. I understood how it propels one forward. I fell in love with people, connection, and friendship more than I had loved myself. And I began to fall in love with myself as I fell in love with college.

Though I often enjoyed my hermit, introverted ways, I continuously learned that I am not a victim. I learned that I have control of my mind, and therefore do not need to be held captive by the dark. I learned that taking small, baby steps does not mean one is behind, or weak. When a child is learning to walk there is no one to compete with, no deadline to meet, and the child is always supported by their innate understanding of the Divine. They have no reason to feel weak or behind. They don't feel shame and are delighted to be going at their own pace. I learned how profound childlikeness is and that I am strong when I tap into childlike patience.

I learned how to be and fell in love with being an artist. I learned that God and my artistic work are intertwined like a silk braid. I live, and breathe, for that gorgeous silk braid that is my life. College is where I grew into myself and I embraced my unique artistry, as a writer and performer. Like a puzzle scattered on the table, all my pieces were there, and eventually after graduating those puzzle pieces began to connect.

As I was looking deeply at myself, digging out all I was not, my professors, and friends, also looked at me deeply, and asked Freeing Beauty to come out. College is where eight-year-old me, fifteen-year-old me, and the emerging young adult me were all invited to come play. Every day I was learning to feel that I am who I am and who I am is enough. I was learning that I am creative, smart, and kind. I was grateful to learn that I am loved by many. Every day I was learning that I am not a perfectly cut gem, but I am my own painted stone, crafted by Soul, glittered with Spirit, and polished by the waters of Truth.

College is where Freeing Beauty became my friend and I let go of all that kept her at bay. Beauty cannot be freed when hatred and doubt are filling the room. Beauty cannot be freed when the light bulbs are burnt out and shattered, and there is no one willing to replace them. I had a lot of cleaning up to do. College is where I began to clean up the hate and doubt. Professors came in and replaced the light bulbs, allowing my wings to warm up, rise from the dust, and let Freeing Beauty emerge in her own time. College brought me home. Thank you, Principia College, friends, and professors alike. There's no turning back.

L.A. Love Affair

California. The Golden State. Los Angeles. The land of new beginnings and abundant opportunity. The city of hope and discovery. The place where all those in search of a brighter tomorrow come to find their calling, or to chase their dreams.

I step out the door for a walk around this new area. I see the city of Los Angeles poised in the distance. Every time I get a glimpse of that cityscape, I think to myself, "I'm in the land of new beginnings!" I take a breath. I ground myself in the awe-inspiring cityscape of L.A.

The sun sets with a kind of peaceful, majesty behind the tall buildings. Oh, Los Angeles, you're gorgeous! I feel my heart well up with joy and my mind simmers on the idea that I live here. My mind rests on the idea that I am finally an adult and I'm living like one. It's like nothing I ever pictured.

Hope, peace, love, passion, wild joy, sweet freedom, fearless creation, discovery without sabotage, heartbreak to healing, wholesome health, independence, courage, confidence, life, peace, and a forever renewing person who is comfortable in her own skin are reflected in the L.A. cityscape as I walk back to where I'm temporarily living.

Dear, beautiful Los Angeles. I don't know how, but from the moment I landed here I can't help but breathe. Your cityscape lights a fire in me and sets my heart at ease. Home has always felt far away because I was always far away from my family. Now that I'm here I'm discovering that I am home in my skin. I am home in creation, in art, and that is the deepest love I can give to you, and to the world. I look at your cityscape glowing in the sunset, and I think, "How did I get here? This is amazing!" Los Angeles, you make me feel all kinds of wonderful. While I haven't found a place of my own yet, I feel so at home looking at you!

As I walk down the sidewalk smelling the jasmine

that wafts through the air, feeling the subtle heat in the breeze and admiring your lovely buildings that stretch above the horizon, I feel every fiber of my being tingle. My heart beats vigorously and yet is totally at peace. My mind feels like a dog chasing his tail and yet is steadfast in confidence that I am in my right place.

    I am in my right place, and grateful for my newfound life as a full-fledged adult! This chapter of my life will be a splendid love affair to remember! I thank you in advance. Look out, Los Angeles! I'm going to take you by storm!

Crawl

Crawl, if you need to. Creep and crawl, if you must, but by all means keep moving. Nature moves gradually through its process of growth and the outcome of its growth is gorgeous. Why? Because it's natural. Nature does and is ruled by nothing but Divine Intuition. The flowers, the sun, the creatures that walk the Earth, and the dirt that crunches under their feet is all working in one accord facilitated by Divine Order.

So naturally their innate blossoming and way of life is gorgeous. From the half inch of a petal flowering to a bird taking its first flight, and the sun shining on all of nature's progress is without total disappointment, or downfall.

Imagine if nature had a jealous streak and an ego, like people do. Imagine if nature could speak its egotistical thoughts, like people do. Flowers, animals, bodies of water, and all other walks of life would not flourish the way they do.

A budding flower would not turn to their fellow bud and say, "How come the roses are blossoming fully? That's not fair. They've had the sun way longer than I have!
Of course they're going to sprout faster than I am. Freaking roses!"

Or in the animal kingdom, a tiger sees a wild boar at the watering hole. She is upset that she can't hunt like her siblings and takes it out on her neighbor. "Excuse me, pig!"

The wild boar corrects the tiger: "Me? I'm a wild boar."

The tiger responds, "Whatever you are, you're not supposed to be here. Whether you're a wild boar, a pig, or just a bore, it doesn't matter. The watering hole is only for predators. So, go find your own water."

The wild boar leaves, feeling hurt.

The tiger continues to herself, "If there was a prize for trash talking and throwing insults, I'd be the champion. It's too bad that doesn't help with hunting; if it did, that dumb wild boar would have been breakfast already. Oh, well...at least he won't see me cry. Geez, I'm a sorry excuse for a tiger."

Or, if a turtle was going about its day walking, trying to get from one place to the other, he wouldn't say, "I can't believe this! I'm trying as hard as I can, but my stupid short legs won't let me go any faster. I feel like a loser. At least no one can see how dumb I look."

Nature is incapable of this self-sabotage. It does not willingly self-destruct. Nature doesn't struggle with feeling small, or insignificant, or fearful, or discontent. Nature does not feel unworthy, or unqualified to take up space. Nature does not overanalyze the space it takes up. It takes the space it needs to grow and nothing around it feels offended. Nature lives moment to moment. There's no agenda, calendar, or sense of time to deter it from what it naturally wants to do and from what it naturally is.

Gradual growth, as seen by nature, is often the most profound and long-lasting way to grow and heal. So, crawl, if you need to. Creep and crawl, if you must, but by all means keep moving.

A New Chapter

Oh, California! Dear Los Angeles, with palm trees galore, blue skies, and air that fills my lungs with vigor, I love you! Yes, I think I can make you home. You, with your succulent jasmine aroma and bright flowers that line every sidewalk. Yes, I think we'll get along just fine.

February brought a feeling of hope and excitement as I arrived in a new place for a new chapter of my life. There was a fresh feeling across the skies of L.A. My eleven-year-old self clashed with my twenty-five-year-old self. Flashes of my eleven-year-old self echoed in me as I navigated this new place. "When I grow up, I'm going to live in California!" I heard her say, overcome with anticipation.

As those words from my young self echoed, my mind flashed forward a few years to my nineteen-year-old self. She was just starting college and more fearful of the world than ever before. She was afraid of herself. She had a hard time making lemonade out of the lemons that life gave her. She didn't want those kinds of lemons, and she didn't want that kind of lemonade, and she didn't want to be the one to do the juicing. So, fear and anger consumed her. California no longer seemed like a fun, exotic place to dream about. Nowhere was fun to dream about. My eleven-year-old self had been long forgotten. College felt like a battleground, and I was not only at war with my schoolwork, but I was also at war with my inner demons on a daily basis. This consumed me for five years and then some. Each year when someone asked what my plans were, I couldn't tell them anything. When someone would ask me where I wanted to live, I couldn't say. Passion had left my being.

Finally, at the ripe age of twenty-three, I graduated from college. I didn't know how to feel. It was hard to process. The cliché saying "The world is your oyster" kept bashing me in the head. *What does that mean? There's no way it could be that great,* I thought. I continued to have brutal battles with my inner demons as I stood on stage at my college graduation. My name was called. It echoed through the auditorium. I began to walk across the stage in my cap, gown, and high-heeled shoes, which had previously given me a blister. I felt my shoulders tense up as I walked, and the blister twisted into my heel like a tiny screw. I thought about how my family was in the audience and my theatre professors were on stage with me, watching as I crossed the stage. Then everyone arrived on the Chapel Green for an outdoor reception. It was beautiful, and yet, I felt so strange in it. I wanted desperately to process this moment with my theatre professors and friends, but there was no time. Everyone was processing their own stuff and full of pride for the day. So, I let it slide and got lost in mingling with people. My parents snapped photos here and there, but there was no time to make sure that they were good. As long as we had some pictures among the chaos of the day then that was fine. At last, the day was over, things were packed, and the next day I made my way home to Connecticut. Things seemed to move really quickly after that. The month of May came to a close and so did my father's piloting career. June went by in a flash and before we knew it mid-July was upon us. My dear childhood home was stripped, almost bare of everything, and packed into boxes. Emotions ran high among the family, and my mind didn't know what to do. The next day I made my way to Michigan for a brief wedding celebration and before I knew it, I landed in Florida, my new home.

    My parents and our dogs had already set up camp within our new home, but my parents came and went over the next six months and so did my pride for my college degree. For six months after graduation, I grappled with my college experience, and how I wished I could feel different. The change of address was not helping my self-esteem, but eventually inevitable growth took over. I celebrated my twenty-fourth birthday in Florida, taking care of the dogs and the house. I had no idea who I was anymore, where I was going, and what made my heart tick. Thinking about getting a job, getting my own place, and where I wanted to live didn't light me up inside one bit. In fact, it made me retreat further into myself. That year was rough, to say the least, but I managed to make it to twenty-five.

Four months after turning twenty-five I arrived in Los Angeles, California. The many years of brutal battles was not quite behind me, but I was stronger when faced with my demons. I was ready for this new chapter away from the hurt, intense isolation, and heartbreak of change. My eleven-year-old self was suddenly revived and teaming up with the maturity of my twenty-five-year-old self. I found myself dreaming up all the ways I wanted to touch the world with my art. I thought about new art and old projects, and it all filled me with life. And there went February.

March was full of promise, as I learned the ropes of adult life and settled into the new job. Dreams of creating art and the joy of making things were still palpable, but then the world broke. Life seemed to come to a screeching halt for everyone around the globe. A sea of unsure times crashed over my newly formed life. This unknown feeling leaked into April.

However, spring has flourished throughout the city and has bathed the streets with gorgeous colors. The air smells sweet like candy and the joy I felt in February lingers whenever I go out for walks.

Oh, California! Dear Los Angeles, I love you! Thank you for being so lovely. I won't give up on this new chapter just yet. Dear Los Angeles, keep spraying your colors, igniting the air with delicious scents, and filling my heart with life. I have hope that things will get better. I look forward to what's ahead.

The Incubator Time

Rough hands, a quiet world, a mind that once refused to change, and a heart turned from putty to a resilient polished stone.

Take care of your hands, just like you've taken care of your heart. The mind is learning to be flexible, which allows for self-care, of all kinds, to blossom. As self-care blossoms then self-love can flourish. Isn't that beautiful? Isn't it natural? It's natural to grow and learn to love who we are. It's natural to find peace in ourselves and our lives.

The amount of time of this journey doesn't matter, as long as we keep moving. There is no definitive destination one has to reach. The peace that one finds in themselves can grow into more peace. The love one finds in themselves can flow from an ego sense of love to a diviner sense of love. A love that is wholesome, not needing attention, and profoundly understood in why it exists.

There may be off days, hard days, moments of disappointment, and times so trying that one comes close to giving up, but because one loves and understands their existence, this allows for a quick recovery from whatever might be testing them. This is the outcome of the heart turned from putty to a resilient polished stone.

This new heart coupled with the new flexible mind is the outcome of our present time. Fear not. This is good. We are in the time of the incubator. The Divine has us wrapped in warm and quiet solitude. She cares for us as we learn to go about our day in a different way. The Divine won't let us fall, or stumble. She loves us like a mother loves her dear baby as they learn how to walk, and so She guides us. As we clumsily put one foot in front of the other, the Divine smiles and stands behind us ready to catch us. No time is spent on the ground because She immediately hoists us on our feet again. The fear of the unknown is momentary because the Divine has given us one mission and that is to *try*. That's all we are asked to do, to try, to learn until we can do it. So, we must do it because there is no other option.

In this time of the incubator there's nothing really to "get through." There's just the present moment full of so much growth and learning. There's only the current moment full of joy, and triumph, and progress, and new discoveries. We are in our right place. The human mind may convince us that this is not what is supposed to happen, but since we have no choice, eventually we get used to our circumstances.

We will be better for this. It's not what we wanted and sometimes we may wish it could go away, but we are not locked in forever. We are not locked in right now! We can go out for a walk and see spring thriving. We can sing a song, or play music, or work on an old project. We can try something new. We can see our family more, or relish in an unfamiliar silence, or dance with vigorous freedom. We can notice how effortlessly the birds sing. We can admire the brilliance of the sun through our window. We can delight in the sensation of our feet on the ground, the breath in our lungs and how it glides out as we exhale. We are not stuck in an incubator. We are not trapped in our beautiful homes, or the temporary room we currently live in. We are alive and living. We are learning that this, to be alive, is enough.

Dancing to Forget

Dancing in the dark hallway alone but feeling watched. My shadow is illuminated by the eerie glow of the red "EXIT" sign and the harsh glare of the floodlight outside. I remember fragments of people I long to be close to and seem to hear the sound of their voices in my tired mind, as I look at the darkened fountain that takes up space outside.

Free and confined at the same time. How can that be? Free to be who I am but confined by my own expectations. Free to work and earn a living but confined by rules and regulations. Free to grow but confined by habit. Free to break habit but confined by resistance. Free but confined at the same time. Free to feel whatever I want but confined by loneliness. Free to be present in my own life but confined by a crippling sense of fear. Fear of trust. Fear of understanding. Fear of sorrow. Fear of myself. Fear of growing up. Fear of loneliness.

Presence in my own life is a frightening idea. To be totally present seems unsatisfying and unearned. Free to be confident but confined by a sense of weakness and worthlessness. The idea of being totally present in my own life seems unsatisfying because I will be proving to people that I can stand on my own feet. To be present in my life means that I am living my own life. If I were present, I might seem strong enough to people. They might feel they could rely on me; some may think I'm so present that I won't have to rely on others. Some may see me as totally present and therefore not needing love, or care. I have grown used to staying slightly off center from total presence. I have grown used to staying slightly disengaged from reality.

Consumed by the dark hallway. Scared and yet fascinated by my own shadow. I dance to find freedom in myself. I dance in an effort to crawl towards joy. I dance to procrastinate. I dance so I won't have to go to bed and face the new day that lies ahead. I dance to escape my feelings and to try to find new ones. I dance to ignite my imagination, to recall the fragments of people I long to see and hear. I dance to forget about myself.

Renewing Color

I come back and renew each day. Small pieces of myself fall away and come back brighter. Like refurbished stained glass, my colors get stronger and bolder.

Growth is beautiful and hellacious at the same time, but in the end it's a gorgeous renewal process. It breathes life into the heart of who we are, our truth, and permeates the good of what gives us our abundant spirit.

Thank God for that! Thank God I can grow and come back. Thank God hell doesn't last forever, and heaven shows its face through the fire. Thank God good is bigger than bad. Thank God I can't stay stuck forever. Thank God I don't have to grow alone. Thank God love persists through the smoke.

What feels grueling in the moment, in the end, becomes soft like silk. Then it fades like dust in the wind. The voices of shame, hurt, anger and discomfort show up with gritted teeth and pierce through one's heart to convince them that they'll never survive the darkness. In the eye of the storm instinct becomes the voice of reason, to remind one to press on. And with that we survive. The harsh inner critic falls like a broken wall, and we rise above the storm.

Thank God for that! Thank God I can come back! Thank God I survive the storm. Thank God the fires of hell die away. Thank God love persists through the smoke. Thank God we can't stay stuck forever.

Beauty and grace, I love you. Heart and soul, we need you, keep going. Love, you are strength. Thank you for holding on like a vice grip. Thank God I can come back!

I love to return to the land of the living! My wings are not meant to be buried forever. Thank God I come back. Thank God my colors renew.

California Palms

This is a sign of my location. These tropical, regal looking trees are a sign to me that I live in California, not just a nursing home in the middle of nowhere. They sway in the breeze among the crystal-clear blue sky. Dear California, keep breathing. Though I haven't seen much of you, since I arrived, there is so much life and sweetness that I've already witnessed. This life I see in nature keeps me going. It keeps my heart beating and hope flowing, that I might one day see more of this lush new home.

It's been rough for the world. I know. It's been hard on all of us. I know. However, there's still life that flows. I look forward to walking down the street and hanging out with friends in a world where masks are not being worn as much. I look forward to breathing the fresh air and delighting in all the sweet smells that perfume the streets.

Though there has been a Great Pause this summer and I have not done all that I thought I would, looking at these trees makes my heart glow. It's a reminder that I did it. My eleven-year-old self was so deeply in love with California that she said, "One day I'm going to live in California!"

As I grew up, I didn't believe it. It didn't seem possible to me and the rational adult that was forming said, "I'm not moving anywhere without a job." However, I was too scared to really look for work. I was listening to my inner critic, the big scary judge and the jury that said, "You're not skilled enough to look for work away from home. You'll never make it! Don't even try!" So, I just waited for something, but I was restless and not sure that any kind of something would come. I prayed. I listened. I waited. I tried to hear my heart. I tried to feel my heart, but it wasn't quite there. Some job options floated to the surface. Some options were in California, but it didn't feel right. I was too scared and bolted to where I was. Then one day something in me decided I was ready to go, anywhere. I looked around, I asked around, and I got a referral. Then I filled out a job application, sent my resume, and wrote my cover letter. All the appropriate grown-up documentation signed and delivered. Then the results. A trial job offer: "How would you like to get paid, have free room and board, and work with children in Los Angeles, California?" was the gist of the offer.

Looking at this job offer every fiber of my being was wrestling with itself. "NO! You're going to freaking mess it up. You're not good enough, or grown up enough, to get something this good and that requires this kind of responsibility." The judge and jury screamed, "Remember McDonald's? That place you said you were going to get a job at because you're not good enough for anything else? That's your destiny — if there is such a thing. You're supposed to live at home, disappoint your parents for eternity, and work at a run-down fast-food place for the rest of your life. This job offer was too easy to get. You don't deserve this." Aside from these comments, I had loving friends, professors, and family to remind me that I'm more than the inner judge and jury. Friends cheered me on. They were excited about this new adventure. Professors gave logical advice, and my family was always there to lend a hand. I'm forever grateful for their gentle love and guidance.

Upon thinking about this move and job offer, my eleven-year-old self returned, reminding me to dream again. Reminding me why, from that young age, I've been in love with California. The Land-of-Make-Believe that made my heart glow, the Land-of-Possibility, full of tropical landscapes, architecture, and creativity. I wanted to be home in myself and my creative life. That's why California always felt like the future home that could give me the creative life I'd dreamed of.

Adults in my life may have tried to deter me from this fantastical dream of living. "So, Barbara, what's on your bucket list?" they asked me.

"Well, I don't have a bucket list, but one thing that I want to do is live in California!" eleven-year-old me replied.

Their faces would contort in seeming disgust. "Ew! Why would you want to live there?" they'd say. "It's full of smoke, it's too hot, and there is always *so much traffic!*"

Feeling unburdened and confident in my unconditional love for California I said, "Well, I still want to live there!" and I left the conversation.

The rational adult and the irrational young dreamer have merged to form this new life and person. It's been strange, exciting, rough, and exhilarating. I made it to the Land-of-Make-Believe. The place where dreamers flock to make something of themselves, or to show others what they've already made of themselves. "This is my art, and my heart, and my soul," says the creative soul, "look if you dare, judge if you must, but sticks and stones have broken these bones, and words can no longer hurt me because this is who I am and where I belong."

California, though I've only seen a small sliver, I delight in you already. I will do my best to wait out this strange shelter-in-place, mask-wearing phase of human existence. It will make for some interesting stories to tell my children and the next generation of kids. Come this fall surely, I will get to reunite with you as myself and explore more of your beauty. Until then, thank you for the palm trees!

Stuck in a Box

I've always been stuck in a box. My feet throb from hitting the ground running. My head pulses from an excess of emotion and a whirlwind of activity. My heart and soul wrestle each other and fight against the outer world. Then they dive inward and fight some more, creating a cycle of perpetual exhaustion and longing.

I've always been stuck in a box. My box floats down an ocean. Sailors, fishermen, and those in their boats out for a joyride see my box floating by. They have no idea there's a living, breathing person inside. In my dark, square container that wanders out at sea, a vast range of emotion fills every corner. The walls are splatter painted with doodles of stories, all my colors, notes to remember, things to say, hopes and dreams that wait to be shared once I'm no longer lost at sea. No one knows all that's inside the box. All they see is a box floating on the water.

No one will know what's inside until they open it. Some have been brave souls and opened my box. These brave souls are friends that have taken time to sit with me and get to know me. They love me regardless of what mood I'm in. Though I may retreat inward most days, they know what's inside. I am very grateful and honored to have friends that open my box during those moments and that lovingly see through the storm. Each of you are precious treasures that are brighter than gold. I'm in awe of your unconditional love.

Most, however, don't know what's inside and don't care to open my box. I must open my own box and step out. Aside from my friends, no one will know the immense challenge it is for me to step out of my box. I curl up like a mouse, in a dark hole, and observe my insides. I nurse every emotion and thought. I observe the outside and pretend I'm living in it while remaining in my box. Sometimes my box is a place of renewal and sanctuary. I need that introverted time to process the world and who I am. Although sometimes my box becomes a pit of despair that drags me into the darkest parts of myself, turning me into a harsh storm with raging thunder clouds and floods of rain. Those that are not my friends, who don't care to open the box, that's fine. You don't have to. You can just stand on the sidelines and watch me open my box, step out, and share my wild creations with you.

I've built my box out of many materials. It started out as a cardboard box that sunk slowly to the bottom of the ocean. Glass cracked too easily and cut those I loved. For that I'm sorry. Wood kept splintering on the inside.

Now my box is made of several materials. I'm not sure of what, but I know it has a strong base and sits on dry land. It's clear, so the sunlight can come in and I'm no longer invisible, although I can draw the blinds when I need to. My box is not heavy, so it can be easily opened.

Perhaps, one day, I won't need a box at all, but for now my isolation is what helps me create, it helps me maintain myself, and love the world without fear. So, I need my box, but I'm not stuck, and I'm no longer lost at sea. However, it still happens sometimes. I'm grateful for my dear golden treasures that bring me back and ground me once again.

Becoming My Best Friend

I'm stuck in this strange cocoon. This strange cocoon can be a training ground for my new life. I can nurture and cultivate a 2.0 version of myself.

This cocoon can give me tools for the future. It may be hard sometimes, but it can be my favorite project. I can be my favorite project.

I can delight in discovering new skills and ways that I like to be. I can find things that I like to do. I can laugh at my burnt meals. I can be grateful for fifth chances and seventh chances that allow me to get better at loving the simple things. I can be grateful for a myriad of do-overs to continue loving myself.

I can listen to my body when it wants more rest and when it needs activity. Resting and activity don't need to be strenuous. I can make my space beautiful and one that I feel happy in.

When the world opens, and humans go back to living more out loud, then I can emerge with stories of my life quarantined in a nursing home. I can share my crazy journey and rejoice in the steps it took to become my best friend.

Jungle Transformation

Transform and transform and transform. Evolve and evolve and evolve. Release. Breathe, release and repeat.

Then sit back and let the smile slowly broaden and brighten. Let the body relax until it can function as it naturally and innately was meant to function and be. Let it be.

You grew up hearing, "Don't force parts." Now, it is time to practice. The practice doesn't require much doing or anything impressive. But release, allow, let. And then transform, transform, and transform. Evolve. Turn over new leaves each moment and each day. The glow of love will emerge on its own time, as long as you don't stop.

Keep moving forward in thought, and activity. Balance will come in time. Let it work on you and come to you. "Don't force parts." Just let expansion happen. Try not to contract, and though the urge will be strong, you know it will not serve in any way. Curling up in a ball does nothing.

So, I ask my heart, to take the wheel. Don't forget to check in with your body and don't let go of the Divine. Tell your mind to trust you, the heart, and the Divine. We are heading into a vast and wild jungle, but transformation is the bold light on the other side.

Releasing Fear

As fear releases, my palate for life expands.
As anguish fades, my horizons broaden.
As tension falls away, breath enters in and my eyes open.
As shame becomes extinguished, love grows and glows like a bright light.
As depression disappears, joy emerges softly.
As anxiety is maintained and diminishes, then peace is free to enter.
As pride crumbles, humility builds a new foundation.
As self-destruction decomposes, self-acceptance takes its place.
As nervousness wears off, presence shows up.
As doubt flees, confidence is ignited.
As distrust of myself and of my Source shatters, trust and security create a new mirror.
As insecurity and belittlement break away, strength gracefully takes center stage.
As fear releases, my palate for life expands.

Florida

Oh, Florida, I forgot how beautiful you are. I forgot how peaceful you are and how beautiful that peace is.

It was hard for me to see the beauty of you and feel grateful for what was in front of me when there was an ocean of fire roaring inside me. I did not feel at home anywhere I went. There were moments of feeling at home in different places, but overall, the ocean kept roaring inside me. So, when I moved to a new home the ocean of fire just got louder. It grew and scorched every fiber of my being. I was exhausted, restless, angry, lonely, anxious, and downright depressed. Home did not exist.

Then I went to California. I thought, *this is it! Here I come to a new life, new adventure, and a place I had dreamed about since I was eleven years old.* Then slowly, like an avalanche, life as the world knew it began to cave in and my world altered too. Each week, each day, felt like trudging through molasses.

The walls of the property I was living in often seemed to turn black and close in on me. With each restriction coming from the outer world, and from my co-workers, my ability to breathe was cut off more each day. Eventually, I began to crumble. Food lost its flavor. Movement felt like pulling myself through that thick and sticky molasses. In and out, up and down. Scrape. Claw. I'd catch my breath, then fall, scrape, claw, and repeat.

My past unresolved battle with myself followed me. It collided brutally with the current pressures and squeezed like a vice grip. Personal and job-related growth appeared through the madness like a whisper, but the ocean of fire was only getting stronger as time moved on.

Friends seemed to disappear or become non-existent. Those that did help were mostly virtual. The world outside seemed to erupt and beg for love. I understood its hardship.

I knew that everyone was going through a hard time. So, it was okay that I had to draw every weapon in my arsenal in an attempt to fight this personal war on my own. A war that had been going on for so long and seemed to get harder to fight with each passing day. Some days were better than others, but my heart always felt bruised, my body always felt singed and depleted, and my mind desperately needed a hug. My mind needed to recharge, but never could. It was constantly working overtime to help my body and my heart, maintain a sense of decorum, and to continuously repair itself at the same time. My mind always stitched itself back together, it would always throw a Band-Aid on that cut, or bandage that wound, while it remained on duty 24/7.

The workday was long. Sometimes fun, but always long. The day would start in the dark. 5:30 a.m. felt like a sucker punch to the gut each day. Somehow, I'd roll out of bed and carved out a quick morning routine for myself. Then by 6:00 or 7:00 a.m. the day seemed to take off like a high-speed train. By 2:30 in the afternoon the train would come to a screeching halt. After a day that felt like speeding down a pitch-black tunnel slide, I would be spit out into the water. SLAP! I'd drag my aching heart and body back to my room. My mind panted, as it gasped for air, "We did it...another day over. Just a couple feet more and I can finally collapse!"

The child in me was desperate to see California, the one she had dreamed about, but she quickly had to grow up. Her survival depended on it. In a short amount of time the child became an adult (on the outside). She got up, she went to work, she did her job as diligently as possible, and maintained a poker face, so that no one could see that inside she was boiling over.

Though I looked like I was functioning I maintained a big secret. This big secret was that as the walls were closing in on me, I was the host of a colossal ocean of fire that burned inside me. No one knew how deeply it burned. No one knew that 5:30 a.m. felt like a sucker punch to the gut each morning. No one knew that 2:30 in the afternoon I would collapse on my bed. No one knew that the weekends were pajama days full of tears. No one knew anything. The cat is out of the bag now.

Right up until the end, my personal war raged on. California, I'm sorry. I don't know if I gave you "the old college try" as they say. I wanted to, but the world didn't let me. I'm sorry it wasn't right for us this time. Maybe, someday... we'll try again.

Florida, you are a sight for sore eyes. I forgot how green your pastures are. I forgot how quiet and serene you can be, even when there is a symphony of farm animals. I forgot how breathtaking your sunsets are and how good it feels to drive down your long roads. Oh, Florida, I didn't think I'd actually miss you, but I did. Now it feels so much better to see you. I learned a thing or two in California that helped me survive. I learned how to cook and experiment with food. I learned that moving my body is good and it is a grounding practice. I've been incorporating those things into my life. While there are still some remnants of the war I faced, I'm beginning to find home in myself. Florida, dear, you are the perfect resting place while I decompress from my head-spinning trip.

I'm grateful for all the information gained while I was on the West Coast. I'm grateful that even through hell, growth is inevitable. I'm grateful that I am beginning to overthrow the ocean of fire, that my mind is regaining its strength, my body is starting to feel comfortable taking up space, my heart is starting to fall in love with itself, and that this reprieve feels like a kiss from Life. I'm grateful to be alive!

Mental Confessions

Dear Self,
I'm sorry.
I'm sorry I stopped you from breathing.
I'm sorry I didn't understand what the body needed.
I'm sorry I didn't take care of you.
I'm sorry I starved you and neglected to nourish you.
I'm sorry I yelled at you and restricted you.
I'm sorry I never celebrated you.
I'll get better.

Dear Self,
I'm sorry.
I'm sorry I never listened to your soul, and to God.
I'm sorry I didn't believe in you, in goodness,
in all that you can do, the lives you can touch,
and that it all comes from Divine Soul, God.
I'm sorry I fought, kicking and screaming, with you.
I'm sorry I pushed back on love, and on God.
I'm sorry I questioned, even surveyed,
every good relationship that presented itself.
I'm sorry I didn't trust you.
I'm sorry that it was easier
to use my imagination as a weapon against you
than to exercise it for good.
I'm sorry I wanted you to break.
I'm sorry I made you feel weighted and drained.
I'm sorry I never let you be
the breath of fresh air you've always wanted to be.
That's going to change...really soon.

Dear Self,
I'm sorry.
I'm sorry I fought with your heart.
I'm sorry I listened to all the innocent teasing
and meaningless comments from siblings.
I'm sorry I used all the teasing
and comments as ammunition.
I'm sorry I spun it all into a huge weapon,
and fired it towards you daily.
I'm sorry I never valued your goodness,
and your emotional intelligence.
I'm sorry I shot you down.
I'll try to let you breathe.

Dear Self,
I'm sorry.
I'm sorry I compared your existence with everyone else's.
I'm sorry I called you a "nobody."
I'm sorry I told you that you needed
to be somebody else, or no one at all.
I'm sorry I told you that existing was invalid
if you couldn't be impressive,
and an expert right away.
I'm sorry I've been so irrational.
I'm sorry I never loved you.
I'm sorry I never cared about you,
unless someone could save you first.
I'm sorry I made self-loathing addictive.
I'm sorry I never let you stand up for yourself.
Please forgive me.

Dear Self,
On my honor
I will try to serve God and you.
To respect you at all times,
and to live by this self-made law.
I know I have work to do.
I'm tempted to be daunted,
and feel like it'll be too hard,
but I want to love you.
I want to be a breath of fresh air
for you and for others.
I want to enter the land of the living
once and for all!
I'm done trying to break.
I'm done weighing everyone down.
That's not living.
It's dying.
I'm sorry that I tried to kill you slowly
and for so long.
Change is coming.
Sincerely,
Your mind

For God

Dear God,
I'm sorry I've been neglecting You
and disbelieving of many things.
I'm sorry that I didn't believe
that I'm whole, complete,
and one hundred percent enough
just as You made me.

Dear God,
I'm sorry.
I'm sorry I let fear and shame,
and embarrassment,
and anger rule my world.
I'm sorry I let negativity rule my life.
I'm sorry I got angry with gratitude,
and that I hated gratitude.
I'm sorry I got angry with myself for just being me.
I'm sorry I was sad, and disappointed to be myself.
I'm sorry that I've wished to be a different person
every day since I was eight years old.

Dear God,
I'm sorry that I've been ungrateful to take a breath
and breathe in all the beauty You have made.
I've been unable to breathe in
Freeing Beauty
and to allow her innate potential
to blossom.
I'm sorry I never believed she had
an abundance of potential
and every second I squashed it.
I'm sorry I made friends with the devil.
I'm sorry my demons made more sense
than any ounce of light You might have given me.

Dear God,
I'm sorry I said "might."
I'm sorry I still side with fear.
I'm sorry love feels so hard to hold onto.
I'm sorry I've fought with You
and blocked You out for so long.
I'm sorry I've forgotten
and have never felt like the little girl
that used to spread her arms out with joy
and say, "God is eberywhere!"
I'm sorry I feel that I've lost that little girl.
I'm sorry I fought with the idea
that You are everywhere.
I'm sorry I've contradicted *so* many things.

Dear God,
I know You are my Source.
I know You are my Origin
and that You could never make a mistake.
I'm working on feeling it
in my heart and my soul
with no room for fear of any kind.
My mind knows that You are Love.
My mind knows that You did not make a mistake
when you created me, your daughter.
My mind knows many of the fundamentals
that I was taught in Sunday School,
but my mind doesn't totally get it,
and my heart and soul don't feel it.

Dear God,
Thank you for your patience.
Thank you for being a constant, unmovable presence in the world.
I'm working on coming back to You with my whole heart,
and my whole soul, and a clear mind.
I'm learning to love the daughter you made
without judgment,
so that I can love the world
with an abundance of trusted love.

Reverse the Character

"Take the costume off," my heart and soul whispered.

I've played a character, one that has had many heavy worries. I've lived in this character most of my life. I've worn her costume for many years. I've worked hard to take it off. Tiny pieces of fabric have come off. It started with the lace from the sleeve cuffs, then the lace from the collar. Perhaps a few buttons fell off along the way, but most of the costume remained. It grew in weight and eventually clung to me like a straitjacket that I got used to.

My heart and soul whispered as they suffocated, "Take the costume off. Open it! Please take the costume off."

The costume took my joy. It ran away with my voice and brainwashed me into feeling intense fear of living for myself. I had grown used to working and living for others. I was the walking dead and I made that my job. I forgot I existed. I forgot I was allowed to just exist.

Heart and soul have whispered long enough. They've had their fill. Today they told me in a loud voice, "Take the costume off. Take the costume off and own your voice because it's your voice!"

Today heart and soul told me in a clear voice, "Take the costume off. Reverse the character. Rewrite your life because it's *your* life. Live *your* life! Love *your* life! LOVE YOURSELF!"

Today I learned that I don't and cannot live for anyone else anymore. Today I learned that those that love me with their whole heart want me to live my life, and not theirs. Those that love me with their whole heart will never leave me. Those that love me with their whole heart will never judge me for speaking up. Those that love me with their whole heart will not be voices of attack that stick to me, but voices of reason, and gentle guiding hands full of love. Those that love me with their whole heart will stand behind me with conviction of my ability to rule my world and with great compassion for how I show up in it. Those that love me with their whole heart will allow me to be myself in totality and not ask me to be someone else so that they can be comfortable.

It's time to reverse the character known as the depressed, anxious victim. It is time to completely take the costume off. It is time to own my voice. It is time to accept the air in my lungs and live life for Life's sake!

Heart and soul can no longer whisper. The cage is damaged. It is time to be Freeing Beauty. She aches for her wings. Love her because she is enough.

As I do this, as I love Freeing Beauty for all she is, then the love from others will not feel so foreign to me. The love from others will feel right, good, and well deserved. I will love Freeing Beauty with my whole heart!

Rescue Me Not

Oh, to be rescued! How inviting it seems. To be rescued is a child's dream, an adolescent desire that was created by Disney, Pixar, and classic fictional stories. It was a great comfort for many years until I had to grow up and face the world. The world that seemed to yell, "Just help yourself!", "Do it yourself!", "Put your big girl panties on and grow up!", "Cry a river, build a bridge, and get over it!"

That same world also gently said, "We all need each other," "That's what friends are for," "I'm here for you," but they also said, "I need space," "We're not that close," "Well, that's life."

How conflicted my child heart and adult mind have felt for years. It's been hard to put the mixed messages together. I grew up dreaming of deep bonds and connections with friends. I went to bed dreaming of that strong man, who went by the name of Prince Charming. Those were wonderful things to think about. Life felt full and rich, but many years of reality slamming itself in my face was painful. As I wrestled with the fact that there's no one on planet Earth that can rescue me, and there's no such thing as Prince Charming, I was forced to question my identity. *What's so great about being an adult? Who am I as a woman without Prince Charming? Why do I have to save myself? It's too hard! It's boring. I don't want to love myself enough to jump into a pile of mud and rescue my own heart and soul. NO! I'm not strong enough. I can't do it. I don't want to do it,* I thought.

I wanted someone else to love me so intensely that they would jump into a pile of mud and save me. But now...I see there's no man strong enough to whisk me away to freedom. I will never be free until I choose to be free. It's up to me to understand what true love feels like with the being I am right now. It's up to me to find emotional balance, and a grounded sense of alignment in myself. It may take a lifetime to achieve this but that's fine. The length of time doesn't matter because I'm beating my own drum. I'm moving at my own pace. I'm going to get there whenever I get there. *Me* and no one else.

Ninety percent of the time it may suck, but then there's that ten percent that shines like a light in the dark. There's that ten percent that feels amazing because I did it by myself, and I did it *for myself!* So, to have Prince Charming would be great, but I don't need him. He'd only get in my way, and perhaps he might even make me feel weak. I've had enough of feeling weak on my own. I don't need anyone else raining on my parade!

To have someone love me intensely and deeply might be nice for a while, but how long would it last? Would it even feel real? Probably not. The only love I need is love of myself, for myself. Some days it may seem totally out of reach, but the only thing that's out of my reach is expecting someone else to be my everything. I'm all I need and that is enough because *I am enough*. So, rescue me not. I can take it from here.

Alignment Gives Us Wings

"Red Bull gives you wings!" someone chimes at the end of each Red Bull advertisement, as some cartoon person sprouts wings and flies away in delight.

However amusing those commercials might be, I bet the energy from drinking Red Bull, or any energy drink, doesn't give one enough energy to feel like they can fly through their day with joy. But what does give a person wings?

Alignment. This alignment is the profound exploration and practice of mental, physical, and emotional peace. By doing this work for ourselves we find a pure, unshakeable wholeness that allows us to be grounded in ourselves, in our lives, and be present in the world for others. This leads us to tap into a world of good. It brings us closer to the Divine.

The world inside us and around us will make much more sense when we align ourselves. This is the greatest gift we can give ourselves and others. It is a finely woven combination of self-love, self-care, and self-discipline that makes this gift of alignment so rich. When we can fine tune this combination of love, care, and discipline for ourselves that's when the gift of alignment really starts to work.

We feel comfortable taking up space in our own bodies, therefore we feel confident taking up space in the world. We feel mentally calm and agile. We can harness our emotion and not let it steamroll over us. We are present and others feel graced by our presence, instead of feeling like they must walk on eggshells around us. Alignment gives us wings!

Letter from Heart and Soul

Showered with love all your life and you couldn't feel it because of the growing demon that became your mind. Interesting...wow.

Showered with love all your life, respected, admired, adored, and praised for just being you and you had no idea because your mind never stopped yelling at you, for being you...and you let it happen. You let your mind talk. You let your mind talk at you. You let every thought it came up with create your identity and you lost yourself to the thoughts at the same time.

Wow. Interesting. So, what's next? Will the battle continue? Will your inner critic keep going? You know it's up to you. Don't let your mind decide this time. Take charge. Please take charge. You know, you are already whole, and always have been. Fear not. Let love happen. Allow the showering of love and respect from those you know happen. Be grateful for it. Feel honored. You are not beneath the respect you get. You are not unworthy of the love that is presented to you. Take it with grace because you have a divine right to take up space. The Divine would never create a beloved child that was broken, or too small to exist. So be humbled by this, and grateful for the love you receive, especially from yourself.

This is no easy task. We know, but it is one that is vital. It is written in the Bible eight times, "Love thy neighbor as thyself." Eight times it says, "Love thy neighbor as thyself." So how can you love those around you if you don't love yourself? Of course, you've never been able to feel the love others have for you, since you've been so horribly disrespectful to yourself. Your mind has given you every reason it can to convince you that love, respect even, is something that you can't give to yourself. Breathe. Keep breathing. Don't stop breathing.

It's time to take charge. You want to take charge.

INCUBATOR LIFE: ON THE ROAD TO FREEING BEAUTY

Your mind has had a long enough turn. It's your turn now. Breathe. Yes, it's your turn now. Starting right now. You are enough.

Your friends,
 Heart and Soul

Negative and Positive Space

When depression, anxiety, discomfort, pain, hate, blame, and all other forms of negativity come to bite, it is often hard not to get swept away. One negative feeling takes us to one negative thought, and another, until we become negative space. We lose sight of who we are at our core. We are *not* negative space. We are *not* darkness. We are positive space. We must accept this and take up the space we occupy. So how do we do this? How do we allow ourselves to be and take up this positive space while negative space feels so overwhelming?

We must affirm the good, the strengths we have, the positive qualities we have, and the good that's around us. Find the shred of light in yourself and others. Then nurture it. *"I am kind. I am loving. I am glad to be alive."* Take nothing for granted. *"I have clean water. I have a place to live. I am important to those who know me."* With these simple positive affirmations, we fill our cup. We fill the positive space. The more we do this, the more we feel good about ourselves and can bring that positive space into the world. Positive space may be difficult to fill, and it may be even harder to keep it filled. However, this is important work. One ounce of negativity in thought, or in the world, can turn into a vast amount of negative space. A small amount of darkness will lead to a stripping away of so much of the good that is at our core. We cannot be both negative space and positive space. We must choose one and commit to it.

Choose. Make a choice to be overcome by darkness or to let the light into your heart. Make a choice to be negative space, the dark storm cloud that brings everyone down. Or be positive space, a true breath of fresh air that is joyous and brings peace. By committing to positive space this does not mean that you must smile all the time or that things will go smoothly, but it is about ownership of all the good you have and can share. It is about being in control of your thoughts, understanding your feelings, and allowing others to feel comfortable around you because of your commitment to positive space. This is not a selfish act. This is an act of love for yourself and for your fellow humans. To commit to negative space is a selfish act. It is unkind to yourself and your fellow human. But it is a choice, and no one can choose for you. It will always be up to you. Choose wisely.

Self-Evaluation and a Call to Greater Action

No one broke your heart. No one broke your spirit. No one was out to get you.

Do you need to blame someone? Do you need to take your anger out on something? Do you need an outlet for the buildup of tension, stress, and restlessness?

Then think of the jerk fear has been. Remember how pride had spun your compassionate nature into something ugly. Wake up to the fact that envy turned you into the Wicked Witch of the West and wreaked havoc on your essence.

Is that not enough? Okay, then look back at how much resentment you held in your heart for the world. It blackened your heart and your mind. Acknowledge how anger has followed you and how you've held its hand. Notice how many times you ached for flattery and manipulated peoples' feelings to get some kind of attention. Did that method of madness ever feel good? Did it feel authentic? Was it an organic, pain-free way of building connections with people? Most likely not.

Be honest. Did your imagination ever represent a loved one accurately? Look closely at how you have deceived yourself and others by holding false ideas, or by idolizing others. It never once served you. It only broke your *own* heart further.

You gave into melancholy, depression, anxiety and so much more. You created an identity around that, and it never once brought you contentment. There was a stinginess to your soul. Cowardice robbed you of your courage.

You waited for material direction and human approval. You planned only how you wanted to feel about certain situations, ones that you had no control over; instead of planning what could help you feel like empowering others, thus using your true joy and essence to ignite the world into being.

You were gluttonous and downright selfish. You thought you could only be fueled by others. You thought inspiration came from a certain outcome, instead of knowing that you originated from a Source more wonderful than can be seen or heard, and therefore had all you needed right in front of you and deep within you. But you constantly fought with it until you forgot how to breathe.

You were lustful for love, attention, and joy. You sought vengeance on God for creating something you thought you had to understand and creating someone you hated to call "yourself." You thought, *how dare God make a mistake like you! How dare She make a voice that doesn't match the face and a body that doesn't work the way humans should!*

From all this you got lazy. You became lazy in your daily efforts, in your life, and in thought. You did not stand up for yourself in any sense of the word. So, you need someone to blame? Then blame that.

Do you need to take your anger out on something? Then take it out on the false character you created and then create a new one.

Do you need an outlet for the buildup of tension, stress, and restlessness? Then acknowledge and deeply consider how you broke your heart with this. Hold it all in your hands with compassion because you didn't know any better, and then decide to do better.

My Oasis

Be here now. Why is it so hard? There is peace all around me. The house, the world, the evening is peaceful and still. The dogs rest close by as I sit on the porch. The sun quietly sets, giving off gentle hints of pink, purple, and orange. The breeze moves slowly, barely tickling the trees, and the next-door farm animals talk amongst themselves. So why is it so hard to be here now?

"Breathe," whispers the breeze. "Breathe."

"I must go," the sun says, "but have no fear, little one. A new day will dawn soon!"

I breathe and enjoy the last moments of light. I take in the springtime air and the fading colors in the sky. The silhouetted trees stand royally around this peaceful oasis. This beautiful oasis that constantly reminds me of Divine Spirit and is a lovely painting of power, grace, and the beauty of Divine Soul.

Though my mind buzzes like an active hive as I fight with my past self, it is only a moment in time. Restless and unhappy I stepped out on the porch. I sat down, looked out at where I'm privileged to currently reside, my oasis, and suddenly the hive inside rested. I found myself here, and well. Grateful for my oasis. Now it is time for a new moment.

Friendship and Connection

Connection of the Heart

My lungs have slowly been learning how to work for the first time. Their natural way of breathing was restricted for many years by harsh thoughts and intense emotions, like a lasso. This lasso was pulled just tight enough to restrict the proper amount of air, but not too tight that my lungs would burst. I was breathing just enough to stay alive, but not enough to function, or feel satisfied about it. I was breathing just enough to stay afloat, but not enough to stay grounded. And so, I went through the world in this way.

My mind is slowly learning how to unwind, but to maintain its shape at the same time. It is used to unraveling like a yarn ball and staying unraveled. When trying to work out a solution to a problem on its own it doesn't know what to do. The yarn ball loses its shape. I reach for the phone and call an outside source for help. The lack of immediate reinforcements leaves me to tend to my own mind. Afraid to face it, like a listless cat to the yarn ball, the ball gets unraveled further. And so, I went through the world in this way.

My emotions are slowly beginning to become more manageable. A low self-esteem led them to be simultaneously suppressed and wildly unleashed. They could be triggered by something as small as the fingernail on your pinky finger due to the buildup of feeling. Trying to comply with a variety of societal views created the perfect pressure cooker. While I boiled and fumed inside, occasionally spilling over, I just barely managed to stay in character. My poker face was decent enough that not many people asked questions. Most that did ask me questions seemed to disregard the answer. And so, I went through the world in this way.

I lost connection with myself and with my Source. I lost my identity because I didn't want to identify with myself. The worst part about this disconnection and loss was that it all was unconscious. It hurt like fire to my skin. It suffocated me like a corset. An unconscious, conditioning corset. Now... my lungs have been learning how to release. My mind has been learning how to release. My emotions have been learning how to act as a tether to my relaxed mind and functioning lungs. By acting as a tether, they find balance and I find strength in myself. Through this profound connection, I learn to love and hold true to my Holy Origin.

Unforgotten Gift

I often long for the past. I long to go back to just a few single moments where certain people were able to hold my glass heart with care. Most of the time I'm required to get a broom after an interaction with someone. No matter how brief the encounter is, I feel I must clean up the glass on the floor and clean the walls of the extra debris that the other spilled.

No one means to spill extra debris, most of the time, but misunderstanding happens. So, I often long to go back to a moment in time when you were there and never made me clean up anything. You were able to hold my glass heart gently. You looked closely at it and saw all my layers of color. You wanted nothing from me, except to see my divine, innate potential. That's why I felt safe sharing my color with you.

I long to go back to those moments as I am now. I want to show you how bright my colors have gotten, how much stronger they are, and some new colors that weren't there before. However, what's done is done. Time moves forward, so I must move forward too, but I won't forget those moments in time. You've left your fingerprints on my heart.

Sometimes my mind replays the memories of those moments when you were gentle, understanding, and nurturing, but in a way that didn't belittle or that might ignite inferiority. Instead, I felt empowered and uplifted. I felt empowered to be myself without shame or need for explanation. I was never required to please you and that allowed for freedom.

Because I was scared, I didn't open myself up, as much as I could have, or as much as I wanted to. I felt like I could be your equal, but there were so many cracks in my glass heart. I didn't know how much authenticity people could handle. I was afraid of broken glass. I stayed guarded just a little.

I always came equipped. Not with weapons. I saved

those for myself, but like Robin Hood with his bow and quiver of arrows, I, too, had tools. I had supplies to protect those with strong exteriors from my vulnerable nature. I was always ready with a broom, a dustpan, and a mop. You might as well just call me the cleaning lady, whose slogan silently echoed inside, "I'll be here 24/7 to explain myself, or clean up any kind of misunderstanding that one might have because I'm the cleaning lady!" I was used to spending lots of time as the cleaning lady.

I compared myself a lot. I was always so grateful that you didn't say, "Don't compare yourself" like everyone else would say. Instead, as gently as you held my heart, you would remind me why I shouldn't compare. You reminded me that the way I showed up, glass heart and all, was needed, wanted, and valued. Thank you! I will always be grateful for that treatment.

From that gift, I was able to value my heart and mind a little more each day. I was able to stop wishing I could be "tough like her" or "a stellar academic like him." Each time you held my heart and delighted in my layers of color I learned to find a friend in myself, and a creative companion in you. I learned to love myself more and began to feel more like your equal each moment.

It was as if you had wrapped my heart with beautiful paper, a nice bow, and handed it back to me with a note that read, "I love you!"

It's rare to be understood on a deep level without judgment. Most people don't try to support or understand like you did. You may not even know what you did, but all I need you to know is that I'm very grateful I know you, and you are special to me.

Most people that I encounter say, "Here's what I think you should do," "Here's how you should feel," or "Don't be like that," which forces me to clean up the mess of their misunderstanding, but you would just sit with me. You would work with me. You would try to understand from your heart, and not your head. You would clean up the mess with me. You met me where I was and walked with me until I (mostly) felt strong enough to stand on my own two feet and celebrate myself. There were moments where you would be firm, but I wasn't afraid of it because I knew I was valued by you.

    I'll keep moving forward since that's all I can do, but I hope one day I can see you again, my creative companion. I hope to create art with you and to show you all my new colors. I hope to show you how much stronger I am, and that my glass heart doesn't break from comparison. I'm still the cleaning lady, ready with her mop in case of misunderstanding, but I don't mind so much anymore because I know that there are people out in the world that see me, and can handle my complete authenticity without fear, or speculation of any kind. Thank you for staying true to yourself and for encouraging me to do the same. I hope one day I can give you the same gift you gave me.

Soul Connections

I've known and come in contact with many people. They all have touched my life in various ways, but they only know certain pieces of who I am. They've only witnessed a select number of things that have shaped me. They only know a few quirks, or a handful of downfalls. No one has seen the whole picture.

No one knows how hard it was to grow into all the layers that make me who I am. No one knows the layers of myself that are forming as we speak, or the layers that are continuously changing color. Not many have seen the intensity, pain, and sweat of my evolution. Not many have understood and taken my hand as I've pushed through stages of torture and battle arenas on my way to finding a sense of home in myself.

Most people that have crossed paths with me have only been able to skim the surface of who I've been and who I'm becoming. When apart or when I've lost touch with someone, they don't get to see the growth that continues. A part of me wishes they could, but it's their loss.

I long to be with someone who can get to know me. I want to know someone that isn't afraid to know me at my core, someone who can see, hear, and love my soul. If only we could meet people from the inside, instead of starting from the outside. However, the world is so superficial that we forget about our hearts. What allows love to keep beating? What brings the color into our world and our life? What helps us create our rich souls? The heart.

To be in action with another, to be totally with them, is like standing on a sailboat as the sky clouds over, the thunder rumbles in the distance, and the ocean begins to churn, forming whitecaps. Instead of trying to reign in the storm, you delight in it. This is true love and deep love of one's soul.

To love every fiber of one's being is to delight in the storm that forms around you as you stand on your sailboat and ride the waves. One wave slaps into another and breaks over the hull of your boat. You don't try to harness any part of the storm because you know it's not about you. The wind that blows, the thunder that crashes like cannon fire and the swirling sea is not a battle that you need to fight, even if your boat takes a beating.

The storm is only fighting itself. You don't need to do anything. Just hold on to your sails and watch as the storm progresses from a dark menace of nature to the most beautiful rainbow that sparkles over a diamond sea.

This is love at its finest. This is the depth of love and humanity. This is the purest form of partnership. This is a wholesome friendship.

I'm grateful to those rare few who could understand that the storm was only about me. I'm grateful to those who could stand on their boat and witness as I wrangled the storm. Thank you for riding the waves with me as the storm becomes a rainbow.

I wish I had more soul connections, but the first step is to connect more with myself. To love myself, and the space I take up, has been an ongoing crusade. It will most likely continue to be an ongoing crusade, but the roughness of the storm will lessen and perhaps parts of the storm will fade.

Some people I've known have needed to sail away and some boats have capsized. I'm sorry I haven't helped you up.

When going through a storm it's hard to notice what's around. Heavy rains get in your eyes, a tidal wave of thoughts that roar like thunder clutter your being and going through the world feels like trying to walk on a raging sea. It's unsettling and beyond difficult.

Those rare few that are able to stand grounded on their sailboats while the storm continuously works itself out are soul connections to me. They don't try to fix or help, unless asked. They have complete faith that I can wrangle the storm and win. They don't comment or judge how I look as I work to find grounding during the storm. They don't ask prompting questions or insist that there are rules to how one must wrangle their own storm. I may not always be working on things in a way that is obvious, but soul connections don't add to the storm. The people that honestly want to be in a friendship or partnership with me know how to ride the waves, with little to no excuses.

To those who capsized but have continuously flipped the boat over and kept riding with me, thank you. I'm grateful you've been trying to keep up. Thank you for working to stay afloat. I will try to keep up with you, but I make no guarantee that my storm is at bay. I'll try to ride yours, if you can keep riding mine. Please don't take offense if I share and dream about a soul connection. My sharing and longing for a soul connection does not mean that you aren't good enough. It does not mean that I don't see you or that I've forgotten about you. It means that I'm on a quest to find a bond with someone that has a boat that won't capsize in the storm. It means that I'm in love with my imagination. It means that my crusade for self-love and joy hasn't been put to rest. It means I'm simultaneously trying to free more color, beauty, and heart. So, skim the surface if you need to. Turn away if you must. Try not to capsize, if you're interested in coming. I need to keep riding. Ride with me! I need a soul connection, or at least someone who doesn't mind capsizing every once in a while.

Hearts

One heart. One heart that works to build itself up each day. One heart that tries to shine and glow. One heart that finds a way to beat and give off heat despite what the world might shout. One heart that keeps going despite what the mind takes on and takes out on the heart. One heart that grows stronger each day. One heart that stays true to itself. One heart that is always complete.

This heart will then love another one day. This heart will find a partner, a mate, who will echo its desires. This heart will love so deeply and purely one day. This heart will feel love so deeply and completely one day. This heart will be able to glow twice as bright. This heart will give openly. This heart will be supported one day. This heart will be humble, wholesome, and grateful. This heart will find passion, and trust. This heart will understand reality in a new way. This heart will love the magic of reality. This heart will be grounded in the world and in love.

Two hearts will unite. These two hearts will bond like a braid. They will weave a colorful blanket with the relationship they create. These two hearts will paint rainbows with their love. They will craft, shape, and sculpt over dark clouds, through skyscrapers, and under flaming bridges. These two hearts will build walls and break them down together. These two hearts will never stop creating and solving together. They will march into hardship and stumble into beauty hand in hand. They will fear nothing. Though fear may try to knock them down, though anger may try to bite, and sadness may try to shake them, there will always be one heart to pick the other up. These two hearts will confide in each other. These two hearts will laugh freely, live authentically, and love passionately. They will balance each other and be unbreakable together. Love will be their foundation, courage will be what they strive for, and joy will be where they rest. These two hearts will find peace together. These two hearts will liquify the darkness and with their love they will pour out beauty.

One heart can survive alone because she finds home within herself. Two hearts will thrive together because they will spark united growth.

Letter to My Best Friend

Dear Best Friend,

When I was younger, around elementary school age, I had a few friends, but I never felt connected to them. I had always longed for a deep connection. I wanted a connection that was so deep that it felt like my heart and the heart of my friend was connected by some kind of electric rope. If lightning could be safely held and stretched out then I wanted to grab it and bolt our hearts together, forever bonded, no matter where we go. I desperately wanted a best friend.

For a while I had a couple of close friends. The three of us did a lot together, but not a lot that made me feel like I was part of the friendship, or that made me feel good about myself. Except Halloween...

For several years my neighbor's mom would buy matching Halloween costumes for us and the three of us would go trick-or-treating together. However, the Halloween costumes, the trick-or-treating, my enthusiasm for the whole Halloween thing, and the friendship between these two girls and myself all ended when I was in third grade.

Each year disconnection would grow, my longing for a best friend would grow, and the idea that it would never happen was convincing. I got used to being alone.

Freshman year of college hit like a gust of wind. I lost myself, and I questioned friendship and connection on a daily basis. I was a raging fire of emotion, heartache, distrust, anxiety, building depression, and much more.

Dear Best Friend, you walked into my world like the gentle kiss of rain. In the freshman dorm, on the same hallway, I was moved by how you and your friends loved my hair. Though I don't remember much from my freshman year of college, I remember you and how good it felt to be surrounded and admired by your friends. I felt loved for things I couldn't control, like my hair. It was so nice.

Through all the trying to make sense of things, the wrestling I did, you became a constant connection. You were always someone I wanted to see. One day I noticed our bond had solidified. I would talk to you frequently. We would hang out on occasion, and we roomed together several times. I found myself feeling so comfortable with you. I felt safe. Though I felt like a menace to myself and society, I felt safe with you.

Though I still worked through my mess, I loved who I was when I was with you. You were not afraid of me. You were grounded in who you were, and in your growth. We both were grounding ourselves and it was exciting! I could hold your hand and you loved to hold mine. You played with my hair and braided it. You didn't mind that I cried, and you waited lovingly for me to get all my emotion out. I never felt judged by you...ever. That was a big deal.

If I was a raging fire then you would be a glistening pond, waiting for me to simmer down and sit next to you. If I was a roaring river then you would be a boulder that would gracefully, but firmly, stop me from gushing any further. I had never smiled brighter, and more confidently, then when I was with you.

Dear Best Friend, you're my girl. I'm so grateful we met when we did. I'm so grateful we have a true and honest friendship. It turns out friendship is real, and better when you're an adult.

I learned a lot about adult friendships when I was in college, but most of what I learned was about myself. Looking back at my college experience, I realize I've come a long way and that what I learned were vital lessons in self-care, how to love myself and how to be patient with others. None of this was easy for me. I put myself through hell and back. I couldn't relax or enjoy very much of what I was doing, but I enjoyed every moment with you.

My elementary school self is blown away by how my life has changed, how I've grown into myself, and that I have a best friend that is beyond any expectation. Before I started college, if someone had told me that at some point during my time there that I would meet a girl from Kenya who would one day become my best friend, the butter to my bread, the color to my blank page, I would not have believed them. I would not have imagined that I'd have a best friend from a totally different country, who was kind, loving, and wonderful in so many ways.

Dear Best Friend, you are beautiful. I love you for your soul, your heart, your kindness, your gentle quiet nature, your fun side, your thick black hair, and your lush chocolate-colored skin. I'm grateful you don't get offended so easily, and you know that I would never hurt you. I'm grateful you're not afraid to see every color that I express. I feel like a masterpiece with you as my best friend.

Somehow life after college has pulled us in different directions, but for the first time in my life the distance doesn't scare me. That is an amazing sign that our friendship is one that can last. For most of my life, I felt like I had to constantly text my friends to maintain a connection. I was afraid they would forget about me. I felt very far away from all my friends, since almost all of them lived somewhere else. I thought the distance and the daily activities my friends had were going to create a break in our connection, and like a rubber band that can easily be snapped, I worried my friends were going to leave me. So, I tried, for many years, to hold on to those people, in an effort to keep the friendship from turning into a rubber band.

For the first time in my life, I don't have to hold on so tightly. I've learned that distance does not dictate connection. I've learned that there must be an equal, and solid give-and-take for a friendship to truly work. But mostly, I've learned that I need a friend who is alive inside, and excited about their own growth. I need a friend who doesn't need me, but instead wants me, and I want them in return. I'm proud to say that for the first time in my life, there is a beautiful and colorful space in my heart shaped like a bolt of lightning. This space, dear Best Friend, is where I hold you in my heart. It is reserved just for you. No one else can touch it and it will never fade. Our hearts are bolted together, and I didn't have to make it happen. It just happened. I'm so grateful. We will continue to work through our separate messes, but we'll get through it together.

Mirror Friends

My friends. My true, honest, humble, grounded, joyous, beautiful, and dear friends, you are forever in my heart. I don't think I can ever stop giving gratitude for you, who you are, and your profound presence in my life. In fact, I think it is my duty to express my gratitude for you, in whatever way I can, until my last breath on this Earth. Perhaps that's excessive, but not to me. Here's why I feel indebted to you for your friendship.

From a young age I squandered my days by trying to destroy myself, so much so that I never felt good in my own skin. I knew deep down that I had a bright soul. I felt alive like fireworks on the Fourth of July when I was by myself and listening to music. I loved to listen to music because I was able to be myself and experience beauty. All I ever wanted was to share the beauty I felt and saw with others.

But soon those moments when I would listen to music behind closed doors were no longer thrilling, at least not in the same way. I stopped wanting to share my feelings, the music, or myself with others. I thought no one would care how I saw the world and I felt very ugly. I began to not feel alive anymore. I no longer felt like fireworks. I became very afraid. I was afraid of everything. I struggled to see the beauty in things, especially in myself. Somewhere in my growing up, I got scared to be me. I was afraid I would be too bright, or too colorful. I didn't want to be too much and therefore unworthy of love. I felt that there was not enough space in the world for many bright and colorful people. I thought that it would be better for me to subdue myself as much as possible so that I wouldn't be too much.

Even though my soul felt loud, colorful, and bright, I very quickly got quiet, dark, and dim. I subdued myself as much as possible and from then on no one could see what I felt on the inside.

No one would ever see what lives inside me. No one will ever see my too much-ness", I thought, "*I should not be taking up too much space. I don't want to overpower anyone. Everyone already feels overpowering to me. It is better that I make myself scarce. Actually, I don't think I should be taking up any space at all. I feel like nobody and everyone else seems to be so much more substantial than I am.*

Eventually I didn't want to be in the world. Being in public was difficult and took a lot of energy. Everywhere I went I felt like a walking mistake. The light of day was hard to face each morning, especially as I began to keep myself awake.

When my family would go to sleep, I would retreat into the darkness of the night and the house. I would simultaneously remove myself from life, make every effort to not have to face daybreak for as long as I could, and I tried to get back in touch with my soul. In the dimly lit room, I would slip my headphones on and fade away. For a while, those moments when I would listen to music alone felt like a refuge. I felt safe behind closed doors, in the dark, and in the music to be as too much, too colorful, and completely myself as I wanted to be.

However, by the time I reached college those nightly music binges became the kiss of death. I exhausted myself. I stopped sleeping. I stopped sleeping so much that morning hurt. My body ached and love felt too impossible to feel. Then I lost my appetite. I got so anxious, and I was so exhausted that I didn't want to eat. I didn't want to do what I loved, and I forgot what I loved. I was running in circles on empty. Emotional adrenaline was all that really fueled me. Until eventually I didn't want to live at all. I thought people would be better off without me. I thought no one needed me or missed me. I thought I only caused discomfort, fear, anger, and exhaustion, that an early death would be a sweet relief to those that knew me. Besides, I was empty. I was nothing. I was useless and insubstantial so why would anyone care if I were gone?

    I wrestled with the boulders I created every day for over a decade. I woke up every day begging to be someone different or to just not be here at all. I wanted to sink and tried to drown by staying up late or all night. I stopped eating regular meals or sometimes anything at all. I tried to engulf myself in the dark. Somehow, no matter how much I wrestled, fought with myself, and hammered away at the boulders, I was unable to completely sink. I could never totally fall into my self-inflicted rabbit hole because like a gentle ray of light there was always a hand that would thrust into the dark and pull me out for a while.

    It was yours, dear friends. You sat with me, talked with me, and I was glad to have the company. Unfortunately, being in the light or even talking about light for too long made me nervous. I always found a way to climb back into my hole and lock the door.

    You amaze me, dear friends! Each moment there was always someone to sweetly hang out with me and gently hold up a mirror in the hole I created. You stayed in that dark hole with me, but because you cared more about me than the dark, you were not overcome by what I was convinced of. You stayed present. You continued to hold up a mirror and remind me that I have a bright soul. No matter how much I got angry, scared, or depressed by my reflection, you were unfazed by my negative reactions.

    You were stubborn and steadfast in showing me the light. You led by example by just going about your day, enjoying life, and being grateful each day that you can take another breath. I admired your shining eyes that looked at me full of hope. I was humbled by your loving messages, but I struggled still when you would hold up that mirror. I hated that mirror. I hated it so much I wanted to break it. I wanted to grab that damn mirror and throw it across the room. Sometimes I would get so angry at your efforts to keep the mirror steady that I tried to push you, dear friends. I tried to yell at you and what I saw in the mirror.

Thank you for gluing your feet to the floor. Thank you for holding that mirror tightly and never giving in to my bouts of emotion. Thank you for knowing who you are, where love comes from, and loving my existence, no matter how much I tried to hate it, or extinguish it. This is why I feel indebted to you. This is why I want to give you the world. This is why I love you deeply. I am forever grateful to call you a friend.

Many friends have left and stopped staying in touch. Perhaps I was too much for them or not enough. At this point I'll never know. What I do know is that they had their own work to do and couldn't wait for me to do mine. They may not have been able to see that during my struggle, I was doing my deep inner work. I broke my own back, but no ego was going to keep me hidden for too long. You had this same conviction. That's why you continued to hold up that clean, simple mirror. Each moment you held up that mirror it was as if you'd smile at me, your eyes would shine, your heart would glow, life would fill your lungs and you'd say, "I see you. I love you. Do you see what I see? Don't be afraid, my friend. I am here. You don't scare me. You are more than your challenges and when you're ready you will see it too. I am here for you always."

Though there were days we didn't talk, I never felt abandoned by you. And what's more is you trusted the work I was doing, and you moved it along by staying present and continuing to love wholeheartedly and unconditionally.

I did the work. I did my own work to belong to myself. I did my own work to understand love, but you stayed with me, as I did the hard-digging work to belong to myself.

You never let go of that mirror, you stayed grounded in your own convictions of how you saw me, and never wavered in who you are. So, while I did my work, I strongly believe that I would not have made it this far without you, dear friends. Without you, I would not have learned when I did, and what I did, from you. Without you, I might still be trying to sink. Instead, I'm practicing how to float on my own. Without you, I might still be internally begging for love, and begging to be someone different. Instead, I'm grateful for the rich love I do have, and glad to be who I am.

I did the work and I continue to do the work, but you, my dear friends, made it possible. You helped me float while I was learning to float on my own. Now I not only practice how to float, but also how to ground myself. For the first time, I'm going to bed before midnight. I'm treating my skin with care. I'm drinking more water. I'm delighting in my body and exercising. I'm learning to eat good meals with lots of nutrients. For the first time in my life, I'm digesting love, peace, joy and happiness. For the first time, I know what it feels like to be truly full. Full without effort. Full, nourished, and satisfied. Full, taking up space, and unafraid.

While this new treatment and outlook to belong to myself feels wonderful, this is all very new. It takes work. Since I conditioned myself to not be, and had tried to disappear for so long, it will take some time for me to make this new treatment a habit, and then a lifestyle, but I will get there.

It is not an easy thing to build someone up, but what you did for me feels special. You built me up not only when I was having a bad day, but on many bad days, when I was purposely trying to sink. When I was trying to not be and figure out how to be, at the same time, there you were with your mirror and lungs full of life. That took energy and work. It took stamina to just be there, even if you didn't have the energy. Thank you.

So, dear friends, I love you and I'm grateful. I look forward to creating new memories together. Ones where we both can be completely ourselves. I look forward to being my own version of the sun and showing up with all my colors. From a laser beam to fireworks, I will be myself, and unafraid because I know you can take it. And as I belong to myself more each day, I look forward to getting to be your friend. I am currently training and getting in shape to be a better friend. A solid, reliable, unwavering friend. I'll be ready with a mirror, grounded and prepared to show up for you one hundred percent.

Creative Prose

The Bird in the Attic

It was springtime and the breeze was blowing. The people who lived in this stuffy, old apartment couldn't tell how beautiful it was outside because the windows were always shut tight. I was just a bird, living in the attic on wallpaper, staring out the window, and dreaming of the day when I could fly like a real bird. I wanted so much to see the world and be free because I knew there was more to me than sticking to wallpaper. I had a purpose in life to fulfill and this was not it.

Life on the wall felt like a waste. I remember getting so excited every time someone would walk into the room. My heart would start pounding and I wanted to yell, "Hey, over here. Open the window!" I would come to life every time a person was present, but when they would leave, and the window was still shut tight, my heart would sink. I yearned to feel the breeze just once, but I never did.

Then one day the family who lived with me was going to leave for spring break. They were going to be out of the house for two weeks. One of the members of the family was a young girl named Scarlet Freeburg and she loved me dearly. She was the only one who knew the truth about who I was, the only one who knew I was alive. Just before the family left on vacation Scarlet got her father, Mr. Freeburg, to go up to the attic. Scarlet walked to the window and stood next to it in protest.

"Why did you bring me up here, honey? We have to go," Mr. Freeburg insisted.

Scarlet said, "Open the window please, Daddy. The white birds need to have air."

"White birds? What white birds?" Mr. Freeburg asked as he looked around the room.

"The ones on the wall!" Scarlet insisted.

After a few moments of resistance, Mr. Freeburg opened the window. I was free to do as I pleased. I couldn't believe it. My heart fluttered faster than ever. I could feel the cool breeze flooding into the room. I felt more alive than I ever had. Suddenly my wings peeled off the wall and my body followed. I was flying! I was so happy that I was laughing inside. This was the greatest day of my life.

"Finally, finally!" I chirped, as I flapped my wings.

I flew out the window as fast as I could. I thought about how Scarlet must have known how badly I wanted my freedom. She knew that I needed a chance to learn how to spread my wings and fly, as every bird deserves.

I traveled the world over the course of those two weeks. I went from New York to Connecticut. Then I went from Connecticut to Massachusetts, to Maine. I went to the Midwest and flew through open fields of grass and blue skies that lasted for miles.

Then I went to California, Oregon, and Washington. The sunny streets of California were so inviting and fun. I wanted to stay there.

In Washington, the White House was so big. I admired its elegance. I hoped to be that elegant one day. I noticed how many people there were in the world and everyone trying to get everywhere. I noticed all the cars that flooded the streets every day, the honking and the fast-paced atmosphere. It was intriguing how no one really wanted to slow down.

Then I flew across the Atlantic Ocean and traveled to Europe. It was amazing! I couldn't believe that I was flying free. I visited London, Germany, and France. I got to stand on top of the Swiss Alps. I felt the breeze run through my feathers as I stood on top of the Swiss mountains. I looked across the mountain range and felt strong. Then I flew to Italy and swam in the beautiful waters of Lake Garda. The water was as blue as the sky. I felt a chill run through my whole body. It felt so good to get wet. I was having so much fun that I forgot I had a home.

I realized that even though I was a bird, and I should be as free as one, I actually had a purpose where I was before, and that purpose was to make people happy being on the wall. As long as I was happy where I was, then people would feel that joy and peace I had and be that way too. Also, I didn't want to worry my dear Scarlet. If I was not home, on the wall, when the Freeburgs got home then I would be in trouble and would have abused my privileges as part of the Freeburg family. I decided it was time to go.

I flew and soared through the skies one last time, across the Atlantic Ocean, and back to my little attic home. My wings gently pasted themselves to the wall, and I eased back onto the wallpaper. I felt invigorated, and at peace, at the same time. I took a breath and let myself sink further into the wall than I ever had before. I felt happy and grateful.

I heard the door slam downstairs. There was shuffling of things and footsteps clomping up the stairs. Mr. Freeburg came into the attic and Scarlet was following close behind. Mr. Freeburg stopped in the middle of the room. It was silent.

Then Scarlet looked at her father. "What is it, Daddy?" she asked.

He smiled softly and said, "I'm glad we left the window open. The room feels fresh and not quite as gloomy, but now that we are home, I'm going to close it. I pay good money for our air-conditioning, and I don't want to waste it."

I watched as Mr. Freeburg closed the window and then walked to the stairs. He called for Scarlet to come with him. Scarlet turned, looked at me, and we took a big breath together. Her eyes gleamed with pride, and she smiled as she took her father's hand. My adventure was over, but I will never forget that it all began when someone left the window open.

Thrill of the Ride

Wood chips under my feet. The bright colored playscape is unfamiliar and foreign, and I feel foreign in it. The shape of each structure is only partly registering in my mind. To stand present with this familiar but hauntingly empty playscape feels like I'm looking at an old friend from a distance. It's there in front of me, and I'm here, but it's not enough. I don't feel connected to it. Something is missing.

    I sit on the swing. I grip the chains and start to go. I can hear myself, from another time, teaching my younger sister how to swing, as I remember the terminology for the thing that gets the swing going. "Pump your legs!" I hear in my head. "Pump! Pump your legs!" I stretch my legs out in front of me and pull them back in. The swing starts to lift me up. Forward and back, forward and back goes the swing. The swing rises just high enough for me to nearly kick the leaves of the trees.

    My mind flashes momentarily to the old swing set in Connecticut. The one that sat in my backyard, in the dirt, surrounded by a rock wall, and a fence with a gate. Trees stood tall and I could pretend I was in my own little forest within the wooded backyard. Like Mary Lennox from The Secret Garden, I had a private forest I could run away to. I could swing high up into the trees, touch the leaves with my feet, and for that moment fear could not touch me. All I cared about was swinging. Back and forth, back and forth, excited to see just how high that little green swing could take me.

    This swing that I'm on now takes me up high but doesn't feel as high as my beloved green swing. I hold onto the chains and feel something happen. A smile spreads across my face. I feel my breath ease out of me like a bus stopping. My breath flows more easily than I thought possible. Just like the swing, my breath flows in and out as my smile brightens across my face.

The colored shapes of the playscape come alive and though it's grey outside, the sun begins to shine in my heart. A soft glow feels as though it's radiating out of me. I fly on the swing and feel my heart fly with it.

How did I so easily forget my childlikeness? It's strange how childhood wasn't that long ago, but it feels so far away. As my heart hardened, and my mind built a hive of noisy thoughts, I quickly forgot about my childhood, but on the swing, flying through the air, I remembered the carefree nature of children, the sweet elasticity of their minds, and their securely open hearts.

Wood chips under my feet again. *Scrape, scrape, scratch.* The swing begins to slow down. It gets slower still. It stops. I take in the thrill of the ride as I stand. I pick up the car keys, and my phone. The playscape loses its life. I'm back to the adult world and feeling like I'm looking at an out-of-date movie. Black and white, and unfamiliar. As I feel the thrill of the ride, I return to a version of myself that's well known, but my heart got a lift for just a moment.

One day, perhaps, the thrill of the ride and being present with my pliable childlike essence will stick, but for now, I'm grateful for the swing set, for it reminded me what I've been missing.

Unleash Your Childlikeness

Pen in hand I write my way through hardship, and document joy. I make contact with my childlikeness. I find the purest parts of myself, and I write away my ugly ego when pen kisses paper.

However, once my pen is down, and the ink no longer flows, it means I have returned to my adult responsibilities. The day fades into an off-putting shade of gray. It has lost its color and I am now slapped with mundane tasks. I walk out into the world of suppressed emotions, and busy schedules where people only know how to operate as human doings, instead of human beings. They step out into the world of doing and return to their oxygen-deprived lives. They lose sleep, and waste energy. They spend money faster than they can make money. But mostly they lose themselves. Somewhere among all the schedule filling, the money spending, and the shoving aside emotions people lose their childlikeness. We trained ourselves to lose it.

Childlikeness: the quality where the soul is ignited, the mind elevated, the heart unafraid to beat, the body simultaneously at peace and fully energized.

Children have bursting personalities and egos that propel them to voice their needs, thus they are the center of attention. But they are innocent, and they only operate the best they know how. However, as they grow, they have a profound sense of adventure and a keen emotional intelligence. They have an extensive imagination and deep love of life. The world they know may move fast at times, but it is not without joy and play. This allows their imaginations to flow, their bodies to work as intended, and their hearts to beat in profound gratitude for being. When they need to, children take their rest without shame.

Shame is something that develops over time. It weakens the heart; it clutters the mind and then it is easily trained into the soul. Once this shame becomes a tangible feeling nothing is ever the same again. Childlikeness is lost. The forever complicating adult world begins.

Adults are forever exhausted, as they try to keep up with their lives, their loved ones, world beliefs, protocol, right vs. wrong, their own ideas, and all the while trying to find something that will make themselves feel whole and energized in a world that is so draining. Often what is found is just an escape because it is easier to maintain an escape for a short time than to accomplish a lifelong dream. An escape allows the adult to take a step towards joy and remember what childlikeness feels like without having to commit to looking foolish, to staying still, or surrendering too much of their ego for too long. Being, for an extended period of time, would be dangerous.

When I begin a Netflix show I understand the safe joy of having an escape. It leaves my heart momentarily separate from responsibility and my mind at rest. But when I begin to write, to put pen, paper, and idea together, I understand the importance of chasing a dream. I touch and tap into my childlikeness. I realize it was never lost, but just needed encouragement. It needed a reason to come out and play. As the ink from my pen flows onto the page I breathe and become a child writing my great adventure story, full of love, mystery, joy, and buckets of fun! As I write this story, I think about sharing it with my classmates and watching their faces light up as they listen. Then connection emerges and everyone comes together in those few moments of sharing. This is life at its best. The world is in living color and how beautiful it is.

My fellow adults, to escape is great, but it is not often something we can aspire to and does not inspire long term peace and growth. Find a reason for being. Something that lets you breathe and ignites your childlike essence. Grab hold of a dream and run with it. Unleash your childlikeness. Leave shame in the dust. Go play!

The Sun, the Moon, and the Stars

The moon shines bright,
as bright as all the stars.
The moon's crescent shape
makes it look like a smile.
Saying, "Goodnight, my love, goodnight.
Sweet dreams, my love, sweet dreams.
I'll be here all night, my love, all night.
I'll be here when the sun comes out to wake you up.
So sweet dreams, my love, goodnight!"

From Spinning to Walking

Spinning in space. Lost in giddy, childlike, all-encompassing joy. Lost in your own world, lost in the music, in the fun of it all, and caressed by safety. Life is sweet, innocent, pure, rich, and inviting. The possibilities feel endless, and you feel full of talent and unafraid of it.

Then at one point you are forced to spin out and stumble into the big wide world of adulthood. Safety feels fleeting and so does everything else. The elixir of music, and all it brought with it, evaporates. Now the floor of life always seems to drop from under you. You are forced to confront reality and it feels like you never seem to stop spinning in space. But don't lose heart. Grab hold of the beauty and innocence that can never be lost and are innate to you.

Fear slithers around you, like a slimy snake. Fear hangs around, like a toxic friend. It holds your hand and whispers insults in your ear, but it doesn't have to keep you captive. Take out your little treasures of beauty and innocence. Hold them close to your heart. Remember those childlike moments of joy, those moments when your heart was beating for the right reasons and your lungs were filled with clean, refreshing life.

Then you can calmly put fear at bay and walk on. Walk on because you can. Walk on because Love lights your path. Walk on because it's your divine right. Walk on.

God's Masterpiece

The sunlight broke through the clouds one last time. Its rays surged through the sky. This form of sunlight contrasted with the stillness of the open field. Time stood still and a masterpiece that could only have been painted by God remained.

I stood alone in this open field that was filled with light and felt myself breathe. Life was my oxygen and all I had to do was allow it to fill me. Ego melted and beauty remained. The clouds seemed to roll in the light. The world was silent, but nature was quietly in motion. Trumpets and soft violins could make up the musical score for this masterpiece.

My thoughts had taken on a stillness of their own. Though the picture of peace painted in front of me was silent, I could hear the trumpets blare, from the way that the light vibrantly broke through the clouds. I could hear the soft violins elegantly playing, from the way the evening breeze tickled the trees. My feet planted on the path, I felt God speak. "Everything will be okay, my dear. Everything is okay." I took a breath.

"Be here now," the picture of peace in front of me said.

And I was. Nature moved me that night, not human will. For the first time I felt the ebb and flow of the Divine. This scene was the essence of harmony. Trees that stood firmly in the ground lined the field like pillars to a courtyard. The lush green grass stuck up straight like brush bristles and the light that broke through the soft clouds was the crown in the silky blue sky.

Nature took up its space with astounding glory. Nothing could compare. I felt small, and yet I took up space. I felt the space I took up and it was enough. There was no war that raged inside. My heart did not ache. My mind did not whirl. My body was not tense. All was well. I was enough.

Dare

Dare to be bold. Dare to be outspoken. Dare to not fit. Dare to be different. Dare to be gentle. Dare to be authentic. Dare to breathe with ease and passion.

Dare to live with valor and vulnerability. Dare to be vulnerable in a world that can't. Dare to feel emotion in a world that is afraid of it. Dare to rein in your emotion with poise and a sense of grace.

Dare to fight. Dare to fight fire with water. Fire can be hot, attractive, and biting, but water is varying in temperature, charming, and aggressive.

Water can knock you down and slap you around at the same time. It can also be gentle and flexible. Water can let go of agenda. Fire maintains its agenda. Fire doesn't easily compromise. Dare to fight fire with water. Dare to be who you are.

Dare to love openly. Dare to be *your* kind of beautiful. Dare to be *your* kind of strong. Dare to be passionate. Dare to defy normality. Dare to create *your* kind of normal.

Dare to embrace. Dare to be observant. Dare to be brave. Dare to see in a different light. Dare to share what you see. Dare to make a safe place by blazing a trail.

Dare to write your truth. Dare to sing what you feel. Dare to dance how you like. Dare to be free of your own inner critic. Dare to be released from others' opinions. Dare to think your thoughts. Dare to share. Dare to speak. Dare to lend a helping hand. Dare to live. Dare to be. Dare to be daring.

Light Befriends the Darkness

Why does Darkness feel so much stronger than Light? Darkness is colorless. Light is so much brighter than Darkness, and yet Darkness feels stronger. Perhaps Darkness seems stronger because he's so wild. He broods, he's restless, and he loves to thrash.

Darkness thrashes while Light is soft. Light comes into the room gently, like the sun that spills in through the window and tickles your face. Morning always comes in gracefully while night just appears. Light has her intense moments. She can get hot and very bright, but she's also steady and quiet. Darkness is loud and even though he might claim that he's unhappy, he loves to listen to himself.

He also loves to compete with Light. "Oh yeah? Well, look how crazy I can get."

Thunder cracks like a cannon ball exploding. Lightning shatters the trees. Birds scatter in terror, and rain slaps the ground.

"What do you think of that?" Darkness chuckles. "I bet you can't do that!"

Light takes a breath. "No, I can't," she admits, "but that's okay." She shines gently on the ground, and it spreads out to the trees and the sky. The birds flock to their nests and sing praises. The grass dances and the trees clap their hands.

Darkness is envious of Light and all the happy attention she gets. So, Darkness begins to brood. He broods all day, trying not to cry, but eventually he can't take all the joy that has fluttered about all day. Rain begins to cover the ground, it floods nests, and thunder shakes the trees. "Why doesn't anybody like ME?" he roars.

Light softly breaks through the ash-colored clouds. She whispers, "Because... sometimes there is more strength in being kind than in gaining attention." Light slowly caresses Darkness. The thunder subsides. Darkness listens to his friend.

Light comforts a little more. She whispers, "And sometimes vulnerability is more powerful than thrashing, crashing or breaking things." The lightning stops. The birds are still, and the trees hold their breath.

"And sometimes humility and love are more important than brooding in fear," Light whispers one last time. "Let us see your authentic self. There's more to you than the storm."

The rain ceases and the clouds break. A sweet breeze glides through the air. Birds tweet in delight and the trees dance with great joy!

"Welcome home," Light says to her friend. "We missed you!"

Embrace the Dirt

Sometimes you have to go through the dirt to appreciate and really feel a sense of growth, progress, and ultimate grounding.

Like a football player grabbing his opponent by the shoulder pads and staring him in the face with sweat dripping down his cheek. That's what we have to do with fear and discomfort. We must embrace the grind. We have to love the grueling, but crucial, moment-to-moment work.

Baby steps. The little things sometimes require all of ourselves. Every ounce of our being is called upon when we need to take a step in a positive direction.

Fear not. The results and big picture come into view here. While baby steps may be painful, they will pay off tomorrow, next month, and for years to come. Just don't stop.

Breathe through it. Hydrate your being. Turn off the monkey mind, the chatter polluting your head. Allow your heart to act as a referee to the mind and body. Emotion will find balance this way and everything will be practicing alignment together.

With this alignment you are armed and ready to head out to the battleground and embrace the grind. So, get your gear in order by getting down in the mud and embracing the dirty mess of doing the work.

I am Freeing Beauty

I have been told that I am unique.
For a while I didn't think that was true,
but now I see I am very unique.
I am my own person,
and I always have been.
I am sweet,
I am nice, and
I think more than anyone else I know.
I have an imagination.
My own style.
I have my own flare,
my own flame.
There are things that I like,
and things that I don't like.
There are things that make me giddy inside,
and things that gross me out.
I am strong and still improving.
God has been so good to me.
He has given me friends
and blessed me with family.
I have talent.
I have courage.
I am beautiful.
My name is Barbara,
and I have many nicknames,
but my true name that sums me up,
that tells YOU who the true Barbara is,
would be Freeing Beauty.
I am Freeing Beauty.
From the core of my being to the clothes on my back,
I am Freeing Beauty.

For a long time, I have had a shell locking me up
and never letting Freeing Beauty out.
But NOW I am out.
I have opened up,
and from this day on it's time
for a new chapter in my life.
There is so much joy I feel right now.
This joy creates a shining force field around me,
and I can't become or go back to the broken,
struggling Barbara that I was when I first met you.
NOW I am Freeing Beauty
And I am all-glorious.

ABOUT THE AUTHOR

Barbara Foster is an interdisciplinary artist. She has written several short stories and poems and has her own blog on her website fosteringcreation.com. Barbara is an actress and has performed in several plays. She has written, produced, and performed a one-woman show. Barbara lives in St. Louis, Missouri.

www.ingramcontent.com/pod-product-compliance
Lightning Source LLC
LaVergne TN
LVHW051924060526
838201LV00060B/4168